CW01676771

Produced by Ashraf Ali

The front cover illustration was done by Aisha Erkaboeva (12)

First Printing, 2019

ISBN 978-1-9160663-0-4

For more orders, please contact:
info@ilmtuition.co.uk
www.ilmtuition.co.uk

Introduction

Reading comprehension is an important skill to develop and can be transferred and used in all areas of learning. This series of comprehension exercises will help your child build vocabulary and deepen their understanding through inferencing and other related skills.

ILM Education's comprehension texts have been carefully selected to include both classic and modern examples ranging from fiction and non-fiction genres.

Unlike most other publications, our guidance section does not just give the answers, it provides detailed evidence from the extract enabling the learners to see for themselves how the solutions were found.

The answers section also shows learners how to figure out the meanings of words from the context. It is not in everyone's interest or ability to memorise the dictionary, but given the right tools and strategies, anyone can make an educated guess at unknown words. Students/parents are reminded of the context and prompted to find clues, giving them a better opportunity to arrive at the correct answer.

This book was produced with students and parents in mind; that is why we have kept it as simple and easy to follow as possible.

This book belongs to

....

Contents

The Wind in the Willows 4

The Railway Children 8

Peter Pan 12

Pinocchio: Master Antonio and the piece of wood 16

Helen Keller 20

Alice in Wonderland 24

Little Women 28

King Arthur's Knights 32

Pinocchio and the Cricket 36

Healthy Breakfast 40

Answers and Guidelines 44

The Wind in the Willows - **Cloze exercise**

Using the context of the passage, fill in the blank spaces with the appropriate word from the selection below.

Meantime the Rat, warm and ____________, dozed by his fireside. His paper of half-finished _______ slipped from his knee, his head fell back, his mouth opened, and he wandered by the _______ banks of dream-rivers. Then a coal ________, the fire crackled and sent up a spurt of flame, and he woke with a start. Remembering what he had been ________ upon, he reached down to the floor for his verses, _______ over them for a minute, and then looked round for the Mole to ask him if he knew a good _____ for something or other.

rhyme	**engaged**	**verdant**	**slipped**	**pored**	**verses**	**comfortable**

The Rat left the house, and carefully _________ the muddy surface of the ground outside, hoping to find the Mole's______. There they were, sure enough. The galoshes were new, just bought for the winter, and the ________ on their soles were fresh and sharp. He could see the _________ of them in the mud, running along straight and purposeful, leading direct to the Wild Wood.

The Rat looked very______ and stood in deep thought for a minute or two. Then he re-entered the house, strapped a belt round his waist, shoved a brace of pistols into it, took up a ______ cudgel that stood in a corner of the hall, and set off for the Wild Wood at a ______ pace.

stout	**pimples**	**grave**	**tracks**	**smart**	**examined**	**imprints**

The Wind in the Willows – Vocab and spelling

Read the comprehension text on the next page and add new and unfamiliar words to the list. Learn the spelling and add a definition that you can remember. Then, write your own sentence with each of the words.

<table>
<tr><th>Word</th><th>Definition/Synonym</th></tr>
<tr><td></td><td></td></tr>
<tr><td colspan="2">Your sentence</td></tr>
<tr><td></td><td></td></tr>
<tr><td colspan="2">Your sentence</td></tr>
<tr><td></td><td></td></tr>
<tr><td colspan="2">Your sentence</td></tr>
<tr><td></td><td></td></tr>
<tr><td colspan="2">Your sentence</td></tr>
<tr><td></td><td></td></tr>
<tr><td colspan="2">Your sentence</td></tr>
<tr><td></td><td></td></tr>
<tr><td colspan="2">Your sentence</td></tr>
</table>

The Wind in The Willows

Originally published in 1908, the book was authored by Kenneth Grahame. In this piece Rat goes out to search for his friend Mole who had gone into the Wild Woods alone.

Meantime the Rat, warm and comfortable, dozed by his fireside. His paper of half-finished verses slipped from his knee, his head fell back, his mouth opened, and he wandered by the verdant banks of dream-rivers. Then a coal slipped, the fire crackled and sent up a spurt of flame, and he woke with a start. Remembering what he had been engaged upon, he reached down to the floor for his verses, pored over them for a minute, and then looked round for the Mole to ask him if he knew a good rhyme for something or other.

But the Mole was not there. He listened for a time. The house seemed very quiet.

Then he called "Moly!" several times, and, receiving no answer, got up and went out into the hall.

The Mole's cap was missing from its accustomed peg. His galoshes, which always lay by the umbrella-stand, were also gone.

The Rat left the house, and carefully examined the muddy surface of the ground outside, hoping to find the Mole's tracks. There they were, sure enough. The galoshes were new, just bought for the winter, and the pimples on their soles were fresh and sharp. He could see the imprints of them in the mud, running along straight and purposeful, leading direct to the Wild Wood.

The Rat looked very grave and stood in deep thought for a minute or two. Then he re-entered the house, strapped a belt round his waist, shoved a brace of pistols into it, took up a stout cudgel that stood in a corner of the hall, and set off for the Wild Wood at a smart pace.

It was already getting towards dusk when he reached the first fringe of trees and plunged without hesitation into the wood, looking anxiously on either side for any sign of his friend. Here and there wicked little faces popped out of holes, but vanished immediately at sight of the valorous animal, his pistols, and the great ugly cudgel in his grasp; and the whistling and pattering, which he had heard quite plainly on his first entry, died away and ceased, and all was very still. He made his way manfully through the length of the wood, to its furthest edge; then, forsaking all paths, he set himself to traverse it, laboriously working over the whole ground, and all the time calling out cheerfully, "Moly, Moly, Moly! Where are you? It's me—it's old Rat!"

He had patiently hunted through the wood for an hour or more, when at last to his joy he heard a little answering cry. Guiding himself by the sound, he made his way through the gathering darkness to the foot of an old beech tree, with a hole in it, and from out of the hole came a feeble voice, saying "Ratty! Is that really you?"

The Rat crept into the hollow, and there he found the Mole, exhausted and still trembling. "O Rat!" he cried, "I've been so frightened, you can't think!"

"O, I quite understand," said the Rat soothingly. "You shouldn't really have gone and done it, Mole. I did my best to keep you from it. We river-bankers, we hardly ever come here by ourselves. If we have to come, we come in couples at least; then we're generally all right. Besides, there are a hundred things one has to know, which we understand all about and you don't, as yet. I mean passwords, and signs, and sayings which have power and effect, and plants you carry in your pocket, and verses you repeat, and dodges and tricks you practise; all simple enough when you know them, but they've got to be known if you're small, or you'll find yourself in trouble. Of course, if you were Badger or Otter, it would be quite another matter."

"Surely the brave Mr Toad wouldn't mind coming here by himself, would he?" inquired the Mole.

"Old Toad?" said the Rat, laughing heartily. "He wouldn't show his face here alone, not for a whole hatful of golden guineas, Toad wouldn't. "

Adapted from *The Wind in the Willows* by Kenneth Grahame

Questions

1. Start means to begin, what does it mean in this phrase: ‘and he woke with a start’? (Line 3) (1)

____

2. What does ‘galoshes’ mean? (Lines 9 and 12) (1)

____

3. What caused imprints in the mud? (1)

____

4. ‘The Rat looked very grave’- what does **grave** mean as it is used in this phrase? (Line 15) (1)

____

5. Why do you think Rat took a pistol and cudgel with him before he went in to the Wild Woods? (1)

____

6. What effect did the pistol and the cudgel have on the animals that were popping their heads out of holes? (1)

____

7. Why do you think Rat was calling out for Mole ‘cheerfully’? (Line 24) (1)

____

8. What sense did Rat use to eventually locate Mole? (1)

____

9. Where do Rat and Mole live? (1)

____

10. What is Rat inferring about Badger and Otter? (1)

____

11. Mr Toad is as brave as Rat- true or false? (1)

____

Total __/11

The Railway Children - **Cloze exercise**

Using the context of the passage, fill in the blank spaces with the appropriate word from the selection below.

There was the table certainly, and there were chairs, but there was no supper. "Let's look in the other rooms," ____ Mother; and they looked. And in each room was the same kind of __________ half-arrangement of furniture, and fire-irons and crockery, and all sorts of odd things on the floor, but there was nothing to eat; even in the ______ there were only a _____ cake-tin and a broken plate with whitening mixed in it. "What a horrid old woman!" said Mother; "she's just walked off with the money and not got us anything to eat at all." "Then ______ we have any supper at all?" asked Phyllis, _________ , stepping back on to a soap-dish that _______ responsively.

pantry	**shan't**	**dismayed**	**rusty**	**cracked**	**blundering**	**said**

Word match

From the passage (The Railway Children), find the word or phrase which most closely corresponds with the word or words on the left.

		Word from text	Look in lines
a	Renewed		1-3
b	Experience		1-3
c	Bleaker		4-6
d	Indeed		9-11
e	Disheartened		16-18
f	Underground room		20-22
g	Tightly		24-26
h	Wax		39-41

The Railway Children- Vocab and spelling

Read the comprehension text on the next page and add new and unfamiliar words to the list. Learn the spelling and add a definition that you can remember. Then, write your own sentence with each of the words.

Word	Definition/Synonym
Your sentence	
Your sentence	
Your sentence	
Your sentence	
Your sentence	
Your sentence	

First published 1906, this extract is from E. Nesbit's 'The Railway Children'.
Roberta, Peter, Phyllis and their mother have just come into their new house and are trying to find their way around.

The Railway Children

She struck a match and relighted the candle and everyone looked at each other by its winky, blinky light.
"Well," she said, "you've often wanted something to happen and now it has. This is quite an adventure, isn't it? I told Mrs. Viney to get us some bread and butter, and meat and things, and to have supper ready. I suppose she's laid it in the dining-room. So let's go and see."
The dining-room opened out of the kitchen. It looked much darker than the kitchen when they went in with the one candle; the kitchen was whitewashed, but the dining-room was dark wood from floor to ceiling, and across the ceiling there were heavy black beams. There was a muddled maze of dusty furniture—the breakfast-room furniture from the old home where they had lived all their lives. It seemed a very long time ago, and a very long way off.
There was the table certainly, and there were chairs, but there was no supper.
"Let's look in the other rooms," said Mother; and they looked. And in each room was the same kind of blundering half-arrangement of furniture, and fire-irons and crockery, and all sorts of odd things on the floor, but there was nothing to eat; even in the pantry there were only a rusty cake-tin and a broken plate with whitening mixed in it.
"What a horrid old woman!" said Mother; "she's just walked off with the money and not got us anything to eat at all."
"Then shan't we have any supper at all?" asked Phyllis, dismayed, stepping back on to a soap-dish that cracked responsively.
"Oh, yes," said Mother, "only it'll mean unpacking one of those big cases that we put in the cellar. Phil, do mind where you're walking to, there's a dear. Peter, hold the light."
The cellar door opened out of the kitchen. There were five wooden steps leading down. It wasn't a proper cellar at all, the children thought, because its ceiling went up as high as the kitchen's. A bacon-rack hung under its ceiling. There was wood in it, and coal. Also the big cases.
Peter held the candle, all on one side, while Mother tried to open the great packing-case. It was very securely nailed down.
"Where's the hammer?" asked Peter.
"That's just it," said Mother. "I'm afraid it's inside the box. But there's a coal-shovel—and there's the kitchen poker."
And with these she tried to get the case open.
"Let me do it," said Peter, thinking he could do it better himself. Everyone thinks this when he sees another person stirring a fire, or opening a box, or untying a knot in a bit of string.
"You'll hurt your hands, Mammy," said Roberta; "let me."
"I wish Father was here," said Phyllis; "he'd get it open in two shakes. What are you kicking me for, Bobbie?"
"I wasn't," said Roberta.
Just then the first of the long nails in the packing-case began to come out with a scrunch. Then a lath was raised and then another, till all four stood up with the long nails in them shining fiercely like iron teeth in the candle-light.
"Hooray!" said Mother; "here are some candles—the very first thing! You girls go and light them. You'll find some saucers and things. Just drop a little candle-grease in the saucer and stick the candle upright in it."

Adapted from *The Railway Children*, by E. Nesbit

Questions

1. What is meant by 'winky, blinky'? (Line 1) (1)

____

2. Why was the dining room darker than the kitchen? (2)

____

____

3. What does the underlined word mean in this phrase?

   a) 'the kitchen was <u>whitewashed</u>' (Line 6) (1)

   ____

   b) 'His bad reputation was **whitewashed**'- what do you think this phrase means? (1)

   ____

4. Who is referred to as a 'horrid woman'? What was she expected to do? (2)

____

____

5. What two words have been contracted to make the word **shan't**? (Line 17) (1)

____

6. What evidence suggests that there was no electricity? (1)

____

7. According to the children, what is a proper cellar like? Mention 2 things. (2)

____

____

Total score__ /11

Peter Pan- Cloze exercise

Mrs Darling first heard of Peter when she was tidying up her children's minds. It is the nightly ______ of every good mother after her children are asleep to ________ in their minds and put things straight for next morning, _________ into their proper places the many articles that have wandered during the day. If you could keep awake (but of course you can't) you would see your own mother doing this, and you would find it very ___________ to watch her. It is quite like tidying up drawers. You would see her on her knees, I expect, lingering humorously over some of your contents, wondering where on earth you had picked this thing up, making ___________ sweet and not so sweet, pressing this to her cheek as if it were as nice as a kitten, and hurriedly _______ that out of_____.

interesting	repacking	rummage	stowing	custom	discoveries	sight

Word match

From the passage (Peter Pan) find the word or phrase which most closely corresponds with the word or words on the left.

		Word from text	Look in lines
a	Ritual		1-3
b	Remaining		4-6
c	Storing		7-9
d	Occasionally		12-14
e	Extremely		12-14
f	Barbarians		16-18
g	For example		24-26
h	Abandoned		28-30
i	Charming		30-32

Peter Pan- Vocab and spelling

Read the comprehension text on the next page and add new and unfamiliar words to the list. Learn the spelling and add a definition that you can remember. Then, write your own sentence with each of the words.

Word	Definition/Synonym
Your sentence	
Your sentence	
Your sentence	
Your sentence	
Your sentence	
Your sentence	

Published as a novel in 1911, 'Peter Pan' is J. M. Barrie's most famous work. The story is about a mischievous yet innocent little boy who can fly and has many adventures on the Island of Neverland that is inhabited by mermaids, fairies, Native Americans and pirates. Other characters include, Tinker Bell, Captain Hook, the Lost Boys, Wendy and her two brothers.
The extract below draws an image of what Neverland may look like.

Peter Pan

Mrs Darling first heard of Peter when she was tidying up her children's minds. It is the nightly custom of every good mother after her children are asleep to rummage in their minds and put things straight for next morning, repacking into their proper places the many articles that have wandered during the day. If you could keep awake (but of course you can't) you would see your own mother doing this, and you would find it very interesting to watch her. It is quite like tidying up drawers. You would see her on her knees, I expect, lingering humorously over some of your contents, wondering where on earth you had picked this thing up, making discoveries sweet and not so sweet, pressing this to her cheek as if it were as nice as a kitten, and hurriedly stowing that out of sight. When you wake in the morning, the naughtiness and evil passions with which you went to bed have been folded up small and placed at the bottom of your mind and on the top, beautifully aired, are spread out our prettier thoughts, ready for you to put on.

I don't know whether you have ever seen a map of a person's mind. Doctors sometimes draw maps of other parts of you, and your own map can become intensely interesting, but catch them trying to draw a map of a child's mind, which is not only confused, but keeps going round all the time. There are zigzag lines on it, just like your temperature on a card, and these are probably roads in the island, for the Neverland is always more or less an island, with astonishing splashes of colour here and there, and coral reefs and rakish-looking craft in the offing, and savages and lonely lairs, and gnomes who are mostly tailors, and caves through which a river runs, and princes with six elder brothers, and a hut fast going to decay, and one very small old lady with a hooked nose. It would be an easy map if that were all, but there is also first day at school, religion, fathers, the round pond, needle-work, murders, hangings, verbs that take the dative, chocolate pudding day, getting into braces, say ninety-nine, three-pence for pulling out your tooth yourself, and so on, and either these are part of the island or they are another map showing through, and it is all rather confusing, especially as nothing will stand still.

Of course, the Neverlands vary a good deal. John's, for instance, had a lagoon with flamingos flying over it at which John was shooting, while Michael, who was very small, had a flamingo with lagoons flying over it. John lived in a boat turned upside down on the sands, Michael in a wigwam, Wendy in a house of leaves deftly sewn together. John had no friends, Michael had friends at night, Wendy had a pet wolf forsaken by its parents, but on the whole, the Neverlands have a family resemblance, and if they stood still in a row you could say of them that they have each other's nose, and so forth. On these magic shores children at play are forever beaching their coracles [small boat]. We too have been there; we can still hear the sound of the surf, though we shall land no more. Of all delectable islands the Neverland is the snuggest and most compact, not large and sprawly, you know, with tedious distances between one adventure and another, but nicely crammed. When you play at it by day with the chairs and table-cloth, it is not in the least alarming, but in the two minutes before you go to sleep it becomes very real. That is why there are night-lights.

Adapted from *Peter Pan* by James M. Barrie

Question

1. At what point of the day or night did Mrs Darling first hear of Peter Pan? (1)

____

2. What is Mrs Darling tidying in her children's minds? (1)

____

3. What simile is used to describe the action of tidying minds? (1)

____

4. Why is it not possible to see your own mother tidying your mind? (from the text) (1)

____

5. Based on the context give an example of:
   a. Discoveries sweet (Line 7) ____________________
   b. And not so sweet (Line 7) ____________________ (2)

6. What does the word intensely mean? (Line 13) (1)

____

7. Why can it be difficult to draw a map of a child's mind? (2)

____

____

8. Where do you think Neverland can be found? (1)

____

Total___/10

Pinocchio: Master Antonio and the piece of wood- **Cloze exercise**

There was once upon a time a piece of wood in the shop of an old _________ named Master Antonio. Everybody, _______ , called him Master Cherry, on account of the end of his nose, which was always as red and ________ as a ripe cherry.

No sooner had Master Cherry set eyes on the piece of wood than his face ______ with delight, and, rubbing his hands together with____________ , he said softly to himself: "This wood has come at the right moment; it will just do to make the leg of a little table."

He immediately took a sharp axe with which to remove the ____ and the rough surface, but just as he was going to give the first stroke he heard a very small voice say___________ , "Do not strike me so hard!"

satisfaction	**carpenter**	**however**	**polished**	**imploringly**	**bark**	**beamed**

Word match

From the passage (Pinocchio) find the word or phrase which most closely corresponds with the word or words on the left.

		Word from text	Look in lines
a	Because of		1-3
b	Glowed		4-6
c	Pleadingly		7-9
d	Apparently		12-14
e	Enormous		14-16
f	Mournfully		16-18
g	Recuperated		19-21
h	Clemency		24-26
i	Dread		35-37

Pinocchio: Master Antonio and the piece of wood- Vocab and spelling

Read the comprehension text on the next page and add new and unfamiliar words to the list. Learn the spelling and add a definition that you can remember. Then, write your own sentence with each of the words.

Word	Definition/Synonym
Your sentence	
Your sentence	
Your sentence	
Your sentence	
Your sentence	
Your sentence	

Pinocchio: Master Antonio and the piece of wood

Written in 1883 by Italian author Carlo Collodi, Pinocchio, is a fictional story about a puppet that comes to life. In this piece the carpenter has a shock of his life when he discovers that a seemingly lifeless piece of wood begins to speak.

There was once upon a time a piece of wood in the shop of an old carpenter named Master Antonio. Everybody, however, called him Master Cherry, on account of the end of his nose, which was always as red and polished as a ripe cherry.

No sooner had Master Cherry set eyes on the piece of wood than his face beamed with delight, and, rubbing his hands together with satisfaction, he said softly to himself:

"This wood has come at the right moment; it will just do to make the leg of a little table."

He immediately took a sharp axe with which to remove the bark and the rough surface, but just as he was going to give the first stroke he heard a very small voice say imploringly, "Do not strike me so hard!"

He turned his terrified eyes all around the room to try and discover where the little voice could possibly have come from, but he saw nobody! He looked under the bench—nobody; he looked into a cupboard that was always shut—nobody; he looked into a basket of shavings and sawdust—nobody; he even opened the door of the shop and gave a glance into the street—and still nobody. Who, then, could it be?

"I see how it is," he said, laughing and scratching his wig, "evidently that little voice was all my imagination. Let us set to work again."

And, taking up the axe, he struck a tremendous blow on the piece of wood.

"Oh! oh! you have hurt me!" cried the same little voice dolefully.

This time Master Cherry was petrified. His eyes started out of his head with fright, his mouth remained open, and his tongue hung out almost to the end of his chin, like a mask on a fountain. As soon as he had recovered the use of his speech he began to say, stuttering and trembling with fear:

"But where on earth can that little voice have come from that said 'Oh! oh!'? Is it possible that this piece of wood could have learned to cry and to lament like a child? I cannot believe it. This piece of wood is nothing but a log for fuel like all the others, and thrown on the fire it would about suffice to boil a saucepan of beans. How then? Can anyone be hidden inside it? If anyone is hidden inside, so much the worse for him. I will settle him at once."

So saying, he seized the poor piece of wood and commenced beating it without mercy against the walls of the room.

Then he stopped to listen if he could hear any little voice lamenting. He waited two minutes—nothing; five minutes—nothing; ten minutes—still nothing!

"I see how it is," he then said, forcing himself to laugh, and pushing up his wig; "evidently the little voice that said 'Oh! oh!' was all my imagination! Let us set to work again."

Putting the axe aside, he took his plane, to plane and polish the bit of wood; but whilst he was running it up and down he heard the same little voice say, laughing:

"Stop! you are tickling me all over!"

This time poor Master Cherry fell down as if he had been struck by lightning. When he at last opened his eyes he found himself seated on the floor.

His face was changed, even the end of his nose, instead of being crimson, as it was nearly always, had become blue from fright.

Pinocchio by Carlo Collodi

Questions

1. Why was Master Antonio referred to as Master Cherry? (1)

___

2. What did he plan on doing with the piece of wood? (1)

___

3. What does imploringly mean? (Line 8) What effect does it have on the speech? (2)

___

___

4. What had happened to Master Cherry's speech for a short time? And why? (2)

___

___

5. Find 3 similes in the extract. (3)

___

___

___

6. In the carpenter's mind, what was the most one could do with that piece of wood? (1)

___

7. Give two pieces of evidence that suggest that the log of wood is small. (2)

___

___

8. What does crimson mean? (Line 36) (1)

___

9. What caused the wood to laugh? (1)

___

Total __/14

Helen Keller- Cloze exercise

At 19 months old Keller __________ an unknown illness described by doctors as "an acute congestion of the stomach and the brain", which might have been scarlet fever or meningitis. The illness left her both ____ and blind. She lived, as she recalled in her______________ , "at sea in a dense fog." At that time, Keller was able to communicate somewhat with Martha Washington, the six-year-old daughter of the family cook, who understood her signs; by the age of seven, Keller had more than 60 home signs to ___________ with her family. Even ______ blind and deaf, Helen Keller had passed through many ________ and she learned to live with her disabilities. She _______ how to tell which person was walking from the _________ of their footsteps.

autobiography	**communicate**	**learned**	**vibrations**	**contracted**	**though**	**obstacles**	**deaf**

Word match

From the passage (Helen Keller) find the word or phrase which most closely corresponds with the word or words on the left.

		Word from text	Look in lines
a	Brothers/ sisters		1-3
b	Ancestry		4-6
c	Resident		4-6
d	Thick		9-11
e	Hurdles		12-14
f	Counselled		16-18
g	Exclusively		24-26
h	Drained		33-35
i	String		38-40

Helen Keller- Vocab and spelling

Read the comprehension text on the next page and add new and unfamiliar words to the list. Learn the spelling and add a definition that you can remember. Then, write your own sentence with each of the words.

<table>
<tr><th>Word</th><th>Definition/Synonym</th></tr>
<tr><td></td><td></td></tr>
<tr><td colspan="2">Your sentence</td></tr>
<tr><td></td><td></td></tr>
<tr><td colspan="2">Your sentence</td></tr>
<tr><td></td><td></td></tr>
<tr><td colspan="2">Your sentence</td></tr>
<tr><td></td><td></td></tr>
<tr><td colspan="2">Your sentence</td></tr>
<tr><td></td><td></td></tr>
<tr><td colspan="2">Your sentence</td></tr>
<tr><td></td><td></td></tr>
<tr><td colspan="2">Your sentence</td></tr>
</table>

Helen Keller

This text is a biography of Helen Keller, it is non-fiction and gives an account of a person's life. Her life is an example of great achievements despite her disabilities.

Helen Adams Keller was born on June 27, 1880, in Tuscumbia, Alabama. She had four siblings; two full siblings, and two older half-brothers from her father's prior marriage.

Her father, Arthur Henley Keller spent many years as an editor of the Tuscumbia *North Alabamian* and had served as a captain in the Confederate Army. Her mother, Catherine Everett (Adams) Keller, was the daughter of Charles W. Adams. Her paternal lineage was traced to Casper Keller, a native of Switzerland.

At 19 months old Keller contracted an unknown illness described by doctors as "an acute congestion of the stomach and the brain", which might have been scarlet fever or meningitis. The illness left her both deaf and blind. She lived, as she recalled in her autobiography, "at sea in a dense fog."

At that time, Keller was able to communicate somewhat with Martha Washington, the six-year-old daughter of the family cook, who understood her signs; by the age of seven, Keller had more than 60 home signs to communicate with her family. Even though blind and deaf, Helen Keller had passed through many obstacles and she learned to live with her disabilities. She learned how to tell which person was walking from the vibrations of their footsteps.

In 1886, young Keller, accompanied by her father, was sent to seek out physician J. Julian Chisolm, an eye, ear, nose, and throat specialist in Baltimore, for advice. Chisholm referred the Kellers to Alexander Graham Bell, who was working with deaf children at the time. Bell advised them to contact the Perkins Institute for the Blind; the school's director asked 20year-old former student Anne Sullivan, herself visually impaired, to become Keller's instructor. It was the beginning of a 49year-long relationship during which Sullivan evolved into Keller's governess and eventually her companion.

Sullivan arrived at Keller's house on March 5, 1887, a day Keller would forever remember as *my soul's birthday*. Sullivan immediately began to teach Helen to communicate by spelling words into her hand, beginning with "d-o-l-l" for the doll that she had brought Keller as a present. Keller was frustrated, at first, because she did not understand that every object had a word uniquely identifying it. In fact, when Sullivan was trying to teach Keller the word for "mug", Keller became so frustrated she broke the mug. Keller's breakthrough in communication came the next month when she realized that the motions her teacher was making on the palm of her hand while running cool water over her other hand, symbolized the idea of "water". Writing in her autobiography, *The Story of My Life,* Keller recalled the moment. "I stood still, my whole attention fixed upon the motions of her fingers. Suddenly I felt a misty consciousness as of something forgotten — a thrill of returning thought; and somehow the mystery of language was revealed to me. I knew then that w-a-t-e-r meant the wonderful cool something that was flowing over my hand. The living word awakened my soul, gave it light, hope, set it free!" Keller then nearly exhausted Sullivan demanding the names of all the other familiar objects in her world.

In 1904, at the age of 24, Keller graduated from Radcliffe, becoming the first deaf-blind person to earn a Bachelor of Arts degree.

Helen wrote many books and articles. She travelled the world giving lectures to raise awareness and raised funds to help deaf and blind people.

Following a series of strokes, Helen spent the later part of her life at home. Helen died in her sleep on 1st June 1968. She was buried at the Washington National Cathedral in Washington, D.C.

Questions

1. How many children did Helen's father, Arthur Henley Keller have? (1)

___

2. List one of Helen's father's jobs. (1)

___

3. What is Helen's maternal grandfather's name? (1)

___

4. What does lineage mean? (Line 5) (1)

___

5. What does Helen mean by 'at sea in a dense fog.'? (Line 9) (2)

___

___

6. How did Keller know who was walking? (1)

___

7. What / who is a physician? (1)

___

8. Who taught Hellen how to communicate using sign? (1)

___

9. Did Anne Sullivan have any disabilities? If yes what was it? (1)

___

10. What is meant by, 'misty consciousness'? (Line 30) (1)

___

11. Today, many people graduate from universities, why was it particularly special of Helen to graduate? (2)

___

___

Total __/13

Alice in Wonderland- **Cloze exercise**

The rabbit-hole went ________ on like a tunnel for some way, and then ______ suddenly down, so suddenly that Alice had not a moment to think about ________ herself before she found herself falling down what seemed to be a very deep well. ______ the well was very deep, or she fell very slowly, for she had plenty of time as she went down to look about her, and to wonder what was going to happen next. First, she tried to look down and make out what she was coming to, but it was too dark to see anything; then she looked at the sides of the well and _______ that they were filled with cupboards and book-shelves: here and there she saw maps and ________ hung upon pegs. She took down a jar from one of the shelves as she passed; it was _______ "ORANGE MARMALADE,"

Either	**dipped**	**straight**	**pictures**	**noticed**	**labelled**	**stopping**

Word match

From the passage (Alice in Wonderland) find the word or phrase which most closely corresponds with the word or words on the left.

		Word from text	Look in lines
a	Peered		1-3
b	Dialogues		1-3
c	Lethargic		4-6
d	Astonishing		7-9
e	Inquisitiveness		11-13
f	Plunged		16-18
g	Dissatisfaction		23-25
h	Speculate		27-29
i	Ambitious		33-35

Alice in Wonderland – Vocab and spelling

Read the comprehension text on the next page and add new and unfamiliar words to the list. Learn the spelling and add a definition that you can remember. Then, write your own sentence with each of the words.

Word	Definition/Synonym
Your sentence	
Your sentence	
Your sentence	
Your sentence	
Your sentence	
Your sentence	

Alice in Wonderland

This fiction story was written in 1865 by Lewis Carroll. In this extract Alice falls down the rabbit-hole.

ALICE was beginning to get very tired of sitting by her sister on the bank, and of having nothing to do: once or twice she had peeped into the book her sister was reading, but it had no pictures or conversations in it, "and what is the use of a book," thought Alice, "without pictures or conversations?"

So she was considering in her own mind (as well as she could, for the hot day made her feel very sleepy and stupid) whether the pleasure of making a daisy-chain would be worth the trouble of getting up and picking the daisies, when suddenly a White Rabbit with pink eyes ran close by her.

There was nothing so *very* remarkable in that; nor did Alice think it so *very* much out of the way to hear the Rabbit say to itself, "Oh dear! Oh dear! I shall be too late!" (when she thought it over afterwards, it occurred to her that she ought to have wondered at this, but at the time it all seemed quite natural); but when the Rabbit actually took a watch out of its waistcoat-pocket, and looked at it, and then hurried on, Alice started to her feet, for it flashed across her mind that she had never before seen a rabbit with either a waistcoat-pocket, or a watch to take out of it, and burning with curiosity, she ran across the field after it, and was just in time to see it pop down a large rabbit-hole under the hedge.

In another moment down went Alice after it, never once considering how in the world she was to get out again.

The rabbit-hole went straight on like a tunnel for some way, and then dipped suddenly down, so suddenly that Alice had not a moment to think about stopping herself before she found herself falling down what seemed to be a very deep well.

Either the well was very deep, or she fell very slowly, for she had plenty of time as she went down to look about her, and to wonder what was going to happen next. First, she tried to look down and make out what she was coming to, but it was too dark to see anything; then she looked at the sides of the well and noticed that they were filled with cupboards and book-shelves: here and there she saw maps and pictures hung upon pegs. She took down a jar from one of the shelves as she passed; it was labelled "ORANGE MARMALADE," but to her disappointment it was empty; she did not like to drop the jar for fear of killing somebody underneath, so managed to put it into one of the cupboards as she fell past it.

"Well!" thought Alice to herself. "After such a fall as this, I shall think nothing of tumbling down stairs! How brave they'll all think me at home! Why, I wouldn't say anything about it, even if I fell off the top of the house!" (Which was very likely true.)

Down, down, down. Would the fall *never* come to an end? "I wonder how many miles I've fallen by this time?" she said aloud. "I must be getting somewhere near the centre of the earth. Let me see: that would be four thousand miles down. I think—" (for, you see, Alice had learnt several things of this sort in her lessons in the schoolroom, and though this was not a very good opportunity for showing off her knowledge, as there was no one to listen to her, still it was good practice to say it over) "—yes, that's about the right distance—but then I wonder what Latitude or Longitude I've got to?" (Alice had no idea what Latitude was, or Longitude either, but thought they were nice grand words to say.)

Adapted from *Alice's Adventures in Wonderland* by Lewis Carroll

Questions

1. Why was Alice not interested in her sister's book? (1)

____

2. What caused Alice to feel lazy and unable to concentrate? (1)

____

3. Find a metaphor. (Lines 11-13) (1)

____

   a. What does this metaphor mean? (1)

____

4. Why would Alice not say anything to anyone even if she fell off the top of the house? (1)

____

5. Find an example of a simile. (1)

____

6. Give two possible reasons why Alice had time to think as she was falling. (2)

____

____

7. Why was it not a good opportunity to show off Alice's knowledge? (1)

____

8.

   a) What use do we have with longitude and latitude? Search online if you need to. (1)

____

   b) Which subject or area of knowledge would you commonly find these words? (1)

____

Total__/11

Little Women- **Cloze exercise**

"I shall get a nice box of Faber's _______ pencils; I really need them," said Amy decidedly. "Mother didn't say anything about our money, and she won't wish us to give up everything. Let's each buy what we want, and have a little fun; I'm sure we work ____ enough to earn it," cried Jo, examining the heels of her shoes in a __________ manner. "I know I do—teaching those ________ children nearly all day, when I'm longing to enjoy myself at home," began Meg, in the __________ tone again. "You don't have half such a hard time as I do," said Jo. "How would you like to be shut up for hours with a nervous, fussy old lady, who keeps you trotting, is never ________, and worries you till you're ready to fly out the __________ or cry?"

tiresome	**hard**	**complaining**	**drawing**	**window**	**satisfied**	**gentlemanly**

Word match

From the passage (Little Women) find the word or phrase which most closely corresponds with the word or words on the left.

		Word from text	Look in lines
a	Happily		3-5
b	Modified		9-11
c	Suggested		9-11
d	Fashion		21-23
e	Defamation		34-36
f	Sarcastic		36-37
g	Pride		36-38
h	Worrying		39-42
i	Disapproving		44-46

Little Women – Vocab and spelling

Read the comprehension text on the next page and add new and unfamiliar words to the list. Learn the spelling and add a definition that you can remember. Then, write your own sentence with each of the words.

Word	Definition/Synonym
Your sentence	
Your sentence	
Your sentence	
Your sentence	
Your sentence	
Your sentence	

Little Women

First published in 1868, this extract is from a novel written by American author Louisa May Alcott. The story follows the lives of four sisters as they grow from children into adults.

"Christmas won't be Christmas without any presents," grumbled Jo, lying on the rug.

"It's so dreadful to be poor!" sighed Meg, looking down at her old dress.

"I don't think it's fair for some girls to have plenty of pretty things, and other girls nothing at all," added little Amy, with an injured sniff.

"We've got Father and Mother, and each other," said Beth contentedly from her corner.

The four young faces on which the firelight shone brightened at the cheerful words, but darkened again as Jo said sadly, "We haven't got Father, and shall not have him for a long time." She didn't say "perhaps never," but each silently added it, thinking of Father far away, where the fighting was.

Nobody spoke for a minute; then Meg said in an altered tone, "You know the reason Mother proposed not having any presents this Christmas was because it is going to be a hard winter for everyone; and she thinks we ought not to spend money for pleasure, when our men are suffering so in the army. We can't do much, but we can make our little sacrifices, and ought to do it gladly. But I am afraid I don't," and Meg shook her head, as she thought regretfully of all the pretty things she wanted.

"But I don't think the little we should spend would do any good. We've each got a dollar, and the army wouldn't be much helped by our giving that. I agree not to expect anything from Mother or you, but I do want to buy *Undine and Sintran* for myself. I've wanted it so long," said Jo, who was a bookworm.

"I planned to spend mine in new music," said Beth, with a little sigh, which no one heard but the hearth brush and kettle-holder.

"I shall get a nice box of Faber's drawing pencils; I really need them," said Amy decidedly.

"Mother didn't say anything about our money, and she won't wish us to give up everything. Let's each buy what we want, and have a little fun; I'm sure we work hard enough to earn it," cried Jo, examining the heels of her shoes in a gentlemanly manner.

"I know I do—teaching those tiresome children nearly all day, when I'm longing to enjoy myself at home," began Meg, in the complaining tone again.

"You don't have half such a hard time as I do," said Jo. "How would you like to be shut up for hours with a nervous, fussy old lady, who keeps you trotting, is never satisfied, and worries you till you're ready to fly out the window or cry?"

"It's naughty to fret, but I do think washing dishes and keeping things tidy is the worst work in the world. It makes me cross, and my hands get so stiff, I can't practice well at all." And Beth looked at her rough hands with a sigh that anyone could hear that time.

"I don't believe any of you suffer as I do," cried Amy, "for you don't have to go to school with impertinent girls, who plague you if you don't know your lessons, and laugh at your dresses, and label your father if he isn't rich, and insult you when your nose isn't nice."

"If you mean libel, I'd say so, and not talk about labels, as if Papa was a pickle bottle," advised Jo, laughing.

"I know what I mean, and you needn't be satirical about it. It's proper to use good words, and improve your vocabulary," returned Amy, with dignity.

"Don't peck at one another, children. Don't you wish we had the money Papa lost when we were little, Jo? Dear me! How happy and good we'd be, if we had no worries!" said Meg, who could remember better times.

"You said the other day you thought we were a deal happier than the King children, for they were fighting and fretting all the time, in spite of their money."

"So I did, Beth. Well, I think we are. For though we do have to work, we make fun of ourselves, and are a pretty jolly set, as Jo would say."

"Jo does use such slang words!" observed Amy, with a reproving look at the long figure stretched on the rug.

Jo immediately sat up, put her hands in her pockets, and began to whistle.

"Don't, Jo. It's so boyish!"

"That's why I do it."

"I detest rude, unladylike girls!"

"I hate affected, niminy-piminy chits!"

Adapted from *Little Women* by Louisa May Alcott

Questions

1. Why did Meg say it is dreadful to be poor? (1)

____

2. Where is father? (1)

____

3. On line 9, 'Meg said in an altered tone': what has the **tone** altered to? (1)

____

4. What are *Undine and Sintram*? Try figuring it out from the text. (1)

____

5. Were the King children rich? (1)

____

6. Why were the girls happier than the King children? (2)

____

____

7. What makes Jo boyish? (1)

____

8. Use a dictionary and find the appropriate meaning of the word 'chit' as it is used in the line 51. (1)

____

9. What are the girls' jobs/or daily activities? What do they do during the day? (4)

____

____

Total__/13

King Arthur's Knights- **Cloze exercise**

'Do you ride back, young Arthur,' he said, 'and fetch me my _____ , for if I do not have it I may not fight.' Willingly Arthur turned his _____ and rode back swiftly. But when he had _______ at the____, he found it shut up and none was within, for all had gone to the jousts. Then was he a little wroth, and rode back _________ how he should ______ a sword for his foster-_______. Suddenly, as he saw the tower of St. Paul's church through the trees, he bethought him of the sword in the stone, about which many men had spoken in his hearing. 'I will ride thither,' said he, 'and see if I may get that sword for my brother, for he shall not be _______ a sword this day.'

brother	**without**	**house**	**arrived**	**obtain**	**horse**	**sword**	**wondering**

Word match

From the passage (King Arthur's Knights) find the word or phrase which most closely corresponds with the word or words on the left.

		Word from text	Look in lines
a	Spectacle		1-3
b	Peculiar		3-5
c	Irritated		5-7
d	Event		14-16
e	Bring		20-22
f	Acquire		23-25
g	Clutched		30-32
h	Out		31
i	Greedy		35-37

King Arthur's Knights – Vocab and spelling

Read the comprehension text on the next page and add new and unfamiliar words to the list. Learn the spelling and add a definition that you can remember. Then, write your own sentence with each of the words.

Word	Definition/Synonym
Your sentence	
Your sentence	
Your sentence	
Your sentence	
Your sentence	
Your sentence	

King Arthur's Knights

This story is based in 6th century England; a time of kings, queens, knights and magicians. So, you will find some unfamiliar words and references that may sound strange to you. But try to guess the meaning from the context. As you read don't forget to draw an image in your mind and try to imagine yourself there.
In this extract people discover the sword in the stone; they try to pull it out to claim the prize of becoming the king.

The clerk ran into the church and told the archbishop, and men were all amazed and would have gone instantly to see this marvel, but the archbishop bade them stay.

'Finish your prayers to God,' he said, 'for no man may touch this strange thing till high Mass be done.'

When Mass was finished, all poured forth from the church and thronged about the stone, and marvelled at the words on the sword. First King Lot, with a light laugh, took hold of the handle and essayed to pull out the point of the sword, but he could not, and his face went hot and angry. Then King Nentres of Garlot took his place with a jest, but though he heaved at the sword with all his burly strength, till it seemed like to snap, he could not move it, and so let go at last with an angry oath. All the others essayed in like manner, but by none was it moved a jot, and all stood about discomfited, looking with black looks at one another and the stone.

'He that is right wise born ruler of Britain is not here,' said the archbishop at length, 'but doubt not he shall come in God's good time. Meanwhile, let a tent be raised over the stone, and do ye lords appoint ten of your number to watch over it, and we will essay the sword again after New Year's Day.'

So that the kings and lords should be kept together, the archbishop appointed a great tournament to be held on New Year's Day on the wasteland north of the city, which men now call Smithfield.

Now when the day was come, a certain lord, Sir Ector de Morven, who had great lands about the isle of Thorney, rode towards the jousts with his son, Sir Kay, and young Arthur, who was Sir Kay's foster-brother. When they had got nearly to the place, suddenly Sir Kay bethought him that he had left his sword at home.

'Do you ride back, young Arthur,' he said, 'and fetch me my sword, for if I do not have it I may not fight.'

Willingly Arthur turned his horse and rode back swiftly. But when he had arrived at the house, he found it shut up and none was within, for all had gone to the jousts. Then was he a little wroth, and rode back wondering how he should obtain a sword for his foster-brother.

Suddenly, as he saw the tower of St. Paul's church through the trees, he bethought him of the sword in the stone, about which many men had spoken in his hearing.

'I will ride thither,' said he, 'and see if I may get that sword for my brother, for he shall not be without a sword this day.'

When he came to the churchyard, he tied his horse to the stile, and went through the grave mounds to the tent wherein was the sword. He found the place unwatched, and the flashing sword was sticking by the point in the stone.

Lightly he grasped the handle of the sword with one hand, and it came forth straightway!

Then, glad that his brother should not be without a sword, he swiftly gat upon his horse and rode on, and delivered the sword to Sir Kay, and thought no more of aught but the splendid knights and richly garbed lords that were at the jousts.

But Sir Kay looked at the sword, and the writing, and knew it was the sword of the stone, and marvelled how young Arthur had possessed himself thereof; and being of a covetous and sour mind he thought how he might take advantage for himself. He went to his father, Sir Ector, and said:

'Lo, father, this is the sword of the stone, and surely am I rightful king.'

Adapted from *King Arthur's Knights: The Tales Re-Told for Boys & Girls* by Henry Gilbert

Questions

1. What is ***Mass*** as it appears in the text? (Line 4) Choose the correct answer. (1)
   a) A large body of matter with no definite shape
   b) Food banquet
   c) A form of Religious worship
   d) A meeting amongst kings

2. What does the word essay/essayed mean as used in the text? (Lines 5 - 13) (1)

   ____

3. When Arthur went back to get the sword, why was no one at home? (1)

   ____

4. What does the word wroth mean? (Line 22) Select the correct answer. (1)

   angry   annoyed   happy   sad

5. '...he swiftly **gat** upon his horse and rode on' (Line 32).
   What does the highlighted word mean? (1)

   ____

6. How were the lords dressed at the jousts? (1)

   ____

7. What does 'Lo' mean? (Line 38) (1)

   ____

8. Did Arthur know about the sword in the stone from before? (1)

   ____

   a. How do you know? (1)

   ____

9. How would you describe Sir Kay? Select two. (2)

   cunning   selfless   selfish   honest

Total ___/11

Pinocchio and the Cricket- **Cloze exercise**

"Woe to those boys who _____ against their parents and run away from home. They will never come to any good in the world, and sooner or _____ they will repent bitterly."

"Sing away, Cricket, as you please, and as long as you please. For me, I have made up my ____ to run away tomorrow at daybreak, because if I remain I shall not escape the _____ of all other boys; I shall be sent to school and shall be made to study either by love or by force. To tell you in confidence, I have no wish to______; it is much more _______ to run after butterflies, or to climb trees and to take the young birds out of their nests."

"Poor little goose! But do you not know that in that way you will grow up a perfect donkey and that everyone will make fun of you?"

"Hold your tongue, you wicked, ill-omened croaker!" _______ Pinocchio.

mind	fate	rebel	amusing	learn	shouted	later

Word match

From the passage (Pinocchio and the Cricket) find the word or phrase which most closely corresponds with the word or words on the left.

		Word from text	Look in lines
a	Attached		1-3
b	A century		9-11
c	misfortune		12-14
d	Revolt		12-14
e	Evade		15-17
f	Cheekiness		24-26
g	wanderer		30-32
h	Fury		38-40
i	Hardly		40-42

Pinocchio and the Cricket - Vocab and spelling

Read the comprehension text on the next page and add new and unfamiliar words to the list. Learn the spelling and add a definition that you can remember. Then, write your own sentence with each of the words.

Word	Definition/Synonym
Your sentence	
Your sentence	
Your sentence	
Your sentence	
Your sentence	
Your sentence	

Pinocchio and the Cricket

Written in 1883 by Italian author Carlo Collodi, Pinocchio, is a fictional story about a puppet that comes to life . In this extract Pinocchio is being advised by a cricket that is old and wise. Find out how Pinocchio responds.

Arriving at the house he found the street door ajar. He pushed it open, went in, and having fastened the latch, threw himself on the floor and gave a great sigh of satisfaction.

But soon he heard someone in the room who was saying:

"Cri-cri-cri!"

"Who calls me?" said Pinocchio in a fright.

"It is I!"

Pinocchio turned round and saw a big cricket crawling slowly up the wall.

"Tell me, Cricket, who may you be?"

"I am the Talking-Cricket, and I have lived in this room a hundred years or more."

"Now, however, this room is mine," said the puppet, "and if you would do me a pleasure go away at once, without even turning round."

"I will not go," answered the Cricket, "until I have told you a great truth."

"Tell it me, then, and be quick about it."

"Woe to those boys who rebel against their parents and run away from home. They will never come to any good in the world, and sooner or later they will repent bitterly."

"Sing away, Cricket, as you please, and as long as you please. For me, I have made up my mind to run away tomorrow at daybreak, because if I remain I shall not escape the fate of all other boys; I shall be sent to school and shall be made to study either by love or by force. To tell you in confidence, I have no wish to learn; it is much more amusing to run after butterflies, or to climb trees and to take the young birds out of their nests."

"Poor little goose! But do you not know that in that way you will grow up a perfect donkey and that everyone will make fun of you?"

"Hold your tongue, you wicked, ill-omened croaker!" shouted Pinocchio.

But the Cricket, who was patient and philosophical, instead of becoming angry at this impertinence, continued in the same tone:

"But if you do not wish to go to school why not at least learn a trade, if only to enable you to earn honestly a piece of bread!"

"Do you want me to tell you?" replied Pinocchio, who was beginning to lose patience. "Amongst all the trades in the world there is only one that really takes my fancy."

"And that trade—what is it?"

"It is to eat, drink, sleep and amuse myself, and to lead a vagabond life from morning to night."

"As a rule," said the Talking-Cricket, "all those who follow that trade end almost always either in a hospital or in prison."

"Take care, you wicked, ill-omened croaker! Woe to you if I fly into a passion!"

"Poor Pinocchio! I really pity you!"

"Why do you pity me?"

"Because you are a puppet and, what is worse, because you have a wooden head."

At these last words Pinocchio jumped up in a rage and, snatching a wooden hammer from the bench, he threw it at the Talking-Cricket.

Perhaps he never meant to hit him, but unfortunately it struck him exactly on the head, so that the poor Cricket had scarcely breath to cry "Cri-cri-cri!" and then he remained dried up and flattened against the wall.

Pinocchio by Carlo Collodi

Questions

1. What does ajar mean? (Line 1) (1)

___

2. Why is Cricket written with a capital letter? (1)

___

3. What literary devise is used in this book with reference to the characters? (1)

___

4. What animal is referenced to indicate someone not very smart? (1)

___

5. What does woe mean? (Line 34) (1)

___

6. What is Pinocchio trying to escape from by running away? (1)

___

7. What other option does Cricket give Pinocchio? And why? (2)

___

8. Describe the Cricket in terms of behaviour and characteristics. (2)

___

9. What happened to Cricket after he was hit? (1)

___

Total __/11

Healthy Breakfast- Cloze exercise

Not hungry first thing in the _______? Pushed for time? Trying to lose______? These _______-counted treats will tempt you to __________ the pleasure of breakfast. From energy-boosting "apple pie" porridge and protein-packed _________ eggs to a nutrient-rich green smoothie and granola bars, there's something for everyone. "________ the habit of eating in the morning is something you can build towards," says dietitian Alison Hornby. "Start off with a light bite, such as a _____ of fruit or low-fat yoghurt.

rediscover	**Creating**	**morning**	**weight**	**scrambled**	**calorie**	**piece**

Word match

From the passage (Healthy Breakfast) find the word or phrase which most closely corresponds with the word or words on the left.

		Word from text	Look in lines
a	Stimulate		1-3
b	Consistent		1-3
c	Entice		4-6
d	Consume		8-10
e	Duties		12-14
f	Soothing		25-27
g	Traditional		26-28
h	Gently cook		27-29
i	Serve up		27-29

Healthy Breakfast - Vocab and spelling

Read the comprehension text on the next page and add new and unfamiliar words to the list. Learn the spelling and add a definition that you can remember. Then, write your own sentence with each of the words.

Word	Definition/Synonym
Your sentence	
Your sentence	
Your sentence	
Your sentence	
Your sentence	
Your sentence	

Healthy breakfasts (for people who hate breakfast)

This article was taken from the NHS website. It provides information on the benefits of having a healthy breakfast and gives tips on how to do that for people who don't like eating first thing in the morning.

Get into the habit of eating a morning meal with these simple breakfasts, designed to whet the appetite of even the most habitual breakfast-skipper.

Not hungry first thing in the morning? Pushed for time? Trying to lose weight? These calorie-counted treats will tempt you to rediscover the pleasure of breakfast.

From energy-boosting "apple pie" porridge and protein-packed scrambled eggs to a nutrient-rich green smoothie and granola bars, there's something for everyone.

"Creating the habit of eating in the morning is something you can build towards," says dietitian Alison Hornby. "Start off with a light bite, such as a piece of fruit or low-fat yoghurt.

"After a while, your morning appetite will naturally increase, and you'll probably find you eat less throughout the day, including snacks."

Research suggests people who eat breakfast are slimmer because they tend to eat less during the day – particularly fewer high-calorie snacks.

If you're short on time in the morning, think about ways to keep your breakfast choice simple. You could also try waking up 10 minutes earlier or getting other chores out of the way ahead of time.

Energy-boosting breakfasts

'Apple pie' porridge

Serves: 1 adult
Preparation time: 10 minutes
Cooking time: 5 minutes
Calories per portion: 315kcal (1,318kJ)

Ingredients

50g porridge oats
200ml semi-skimmed milk
1 medium dessert apple, diced
Pinch of cinnamon

This is a warm, comforting porridge spiced up with the classic flavours of a homemade apple pie.

Throw all the ingredients into a saucepan. Heat and stir until boiling, then lower the heat and simmer gently for 5 minutes, stirring often.

Spoon the porridge into a serving bowl and add a sprinkle of cinnamon.

Questions

1. What does the word 'habitual' mean? (Line 2) (1)

____

2. What does 'whet the appetite' mean? (1)

____

3. In the above article there is only one recipe, which word/phrase tells you that there were more recipes? (1)

____

4. What habit will cause your appetite to increase? (1)

____

5. Why are breakfast eaters slimmer? (1)

____

6. Find an example of an alliteration. (Lines 4-9) (1)

____

7. What does the word simmer mean? (Line 27) (1)

____

8. If you are short of time, what two things could you do to help you have breakfast?

   a. ______________________

   b. ______________________ (2)

Total __/9

Answers and Guidelines

The Wind in The Willows

Cloze exercise- check answers against the main text.

Comprehension Answers
Mind picture
This book was written over 100 years ago, so consider how the language or reference to certain things will differ to modern-day usage.
Rat is at home, warm and cosy. When he wakes up, he realises that his friend Mole has gone. Rat is extremely concerned for Mole as he realises that Mole has wandered off into the Wild Woods (an unfamiliar and hostile place).
The characters are Rat and Mole- the animals are given human characteristics.
Can you imagine the animals speaking, wearing clothes and behaving as humans do?
This is called **anthropomorphism** (when animals and objects do human things) think of Scooby-Doo and other cartoon characters you might have seen.
Rat is depicted as being brave and ready to rescue his friend, while Mole is nervous and timid, out of his depths in the Wild Woods.

> **The Wind in The Willows**
>
> Originally published in 1908, the book was authored by Kenneth Grahame. In this piece Rat goes out to search for his friend Mole who had gone into the Wild Woods alone.
>
> Meantime the Rat, warm and comfortable, dozed by his fireside. His paper of half-finished verses slipped from his knee, his head fell back, his mouth opened, and he wandered by the verdant banks of dream-rivers. Then a coal slipped, the fire crackled and sent up a spurt of flame, and he woke with a start. Remembering what he had been engaged upon, he reached down to the floor for his verses, pored over them for a minute, and then looked round for the Mole to ask him if he knew a good rhyme for something or other.
> But the Mole was not there. He listened for a time. The house seemed very quiet.
> Then he called "Moly!" several times, and, receiving no answer, got up and went out into the hall.
> The Mole's cap was missing from its accustomed peg. His galoshes, which always lay by the umbrella-stand, were also gone.
> The Rat left the house, and carefully examined the muddy surface of the ground outside, hoping to find the Mole's tracks. There they were, sure enough. The galoshes were new, just bought for the winter, and the pimples on their soles were fresh and sharp. He could see the imprints of them in the mud, running along straight and purposeful, leading direct to the Wild Wood.
> The Rat looked very grave, and stood in deep thought for a minute or two. Then he re-entered the house, strapped a belt round his waist, shoved a brace of pistols into it, took up a stout cudgel that stood in a corner of the hall, and set off for the Wild Wood at a smart pace.

1. Start means to begin, what does it mean in this phrase: 'and he woke with a start'? (Line 3)
Answer: Jump /startle/twitch
Think about what just happened. Rat is asleep, then a piece of coal fell in the fire and caused the flames to rise, making a noise. This made Rate wake up with a *start/jump/ twitch* – (as he is startled by the sound)
When someone is awoken by a sudden noise, it may cause them to be startled or wake up with a jump.

2. What does 'galoshes' mean? (Lines 9 and 12)
Answer*:* Waterproof shoes/ wellies /rubber overshoes/ footwear (any one)
Here, Rat is looking for Mole's cap and galoshes by the peg and umbrella stand. What would you find near the front door where you keep outdoor clothing/equipment?
What item has 'pimples on their sole' and can leave imprints in the mud?

3. What caused imprints in the mud?
Answer: Pimples on the soles of the galoshes.

4. 'The Rat looked very grave'- what does '**grave**' mean as it is used in this phrase? (Line 15)
Answer: Serious
If you didn't already know the meaning, then consider what is happening in the sentences before and after.
a. Rat is very **concerned** that Mole has wandered off into the Wild Woods and then afterwards he goes indoors and prepares himself with weapons- so he's about to do something **serious**.
b. Consider the word in the sentence itself. The word '**grave**' is used to describe how the Rat looked. Therefore, it is an adjective- describing the way he looked. -'The Rat looked very ***serious***'.

5. Why do you think Rat took a pistol and cudgel with him before he went into the Wild Woods?
Answer: For protection/ defence against unknown creatures in the woods/safety reasons.
Although it is not explicit in the text, we can infer that it was for protection and self-defence. The Wild Woods has been depicted as a hostile environment; with many dangers lurking in the darkness, it is necessary to take precautions, especially for small animals such as Rat and Mole.

corner of the hall, and set off for the Wild Wood at a smart pace.

It was already getting towards dusk when he reached the first fringe of trees and plunged without hesitation into the wood, looking anxiously on either side for any sign of his friend. Here and there wicked little faces popped out of holes, but vanished immediately at sight of the valorous animal, his pistols, and the great ugly cudgel in his grasp; and the whistling and pattering, which he had heard quite plainly on his first entry, died away and ceased, and all was very still. He made his way manfully through the length of the wood, to its furthest edge; then, forsaking all paths, he set himself to traverse it, laboriously working over the whole ground, and all the time calling out cheerfully, "Moly, Moly, Moly! Where are you? It's me—it's old Rat!"

He had patiently hunted through the wood for an hour or more, when at last to his joy he heard a little answering cry. Guiding himself by the sound, he made his way through the gathering darkness to the foot of an old beech tree, with a hole in it, and from out of the hole came a feeble voice, saying "Ratty! Is that really you?"

The Rat crept into the hollow, and there he found the Mole, exhausted and still trembling. "O Rat!" he cried, "I've been so frightened, you can't think!"

"O, I quite understand," said the Rat soothingly. "You shouldn't really have gone and done it, Mole. I did my best to keep you from it. We river-bankers, we hardly ever come here by ourselves. If we have to come, we come in couples at least; then we're generally all right. Besides, there are a hundred things one has to know, which we understand all about and you don't, as yet. I mean passwords, and signs, and sayings which have power and effect, and plants you carry in your pocket, and verses you repeat, and dodges and tricks you practise; all simple enough when you know them, but they've got to be known if you're small, or you'll find yourself in trouble. Of course, if you were Badger or Otter, it would be quite another matter."

"Surely the brave Mr Toad wouldn't mind coming here by himself, would he?" inquired the Mole.

"Old Toad?" said the Rat, laughing heartily. "He wouldn't show his face here alone, not for a whole hatful of golden guineas, Toad wouldn't. "

Adapted from *The Wind in the Willows* by Kenneth Grahame

6. What effect did the pistol and the cudgel have on the animals that were popping their heads out of holes?
Answer: It caused the animals to hide out of fear of the weapons.
(Lines 19-21)

7. Why do you think Rat was calling out for Mole 'cheerfully'? (Line 24)
Answer: To keep his morale high/ show a confident front / it could be for the benefit of Mole as a way of reassurance for his friend.

There isn't much explanation as to why he was calling out cheerfully. But perhaps it was to keep his spirits high or to offer reassurance to Mole, who, of course, is very scared in the Wild Woods.

How would you feel if you were in Rat's situation?
Would you be scared? What would you do to keep your spirits high?

8. What sense did Rat use to eventually locate Mole?
Answer: Hearing/ sound (Lines 26-27)

9. Where do Rat and Mole live?
Answer: By the riverbank

10. What is Rat inferring about Badger and Otter?
Answer: They are bigger.

Rat mentions certain strategies to stay safe in the woods. He says it's necessary to know these, especially for smaller animals. Rat then goes on to say that Badger and Otter wouldn't have any problems- suggesting that Badger and Otter are bigger. (Lines 37-38)

11. Mr Toad is as brave as Rat- true or false?
Answer: False (Lines 40-41)

The Railway Children

Word match

a) Relighted b) Adventure c) Darker d) Certainly e) Dismayed f) Cellar g) Securely h) Grease

Comprehension

Mind picture

Firstly, let's draw a picture of the setting and the characters in our minds.

The characters- Three children and their mother.

They have just entered their new house. They have travelled from their old home; although we don't know the distance, we can assume they must be tired and hungry. As this is a new place, the children must be a little anxious and worried, especially as it is late at night and dark in an unfamiliar place. They stumble through the house by candlelight in search of their supper.

As you answered the questions, the details of your mind picture should grow clearer. You should imagine the scene for each of the rooms- the kitchen, dining room and cellar.

First published 1906, this extract is from E. Nesbit's 'The Railway Children'.
Roberta, Peter, Phyllis and their mother have just come into their new house and are trying to find their way around.

The Railway Children

She struck a match and relighted the candle and everyone looked at each other by its winky, blinky light. "Well," she said, "you've often wanted something to happen and now it has. This is quite an adventure, isn't it? I told Mrs. Viney to get us some bread and butter, and meat and things, and to have supper ready. I suppose she's laid it in the dining-room. So let's go and see." The dining-room opened out of the kitchen. It looked much darker than the kitchen when they went in with the one candle; the kitchen was whitewashed, but the dining-room was dark wood from floor to ceiling, and across the ceiling there were heavy black beams. There was a muddled maze of dusty furniture—the breakfast-room furniture from the old home where they had lived all their lives. It seemed a very long time ago, and a very long way off.

There was the table certainly, and there were chairs, but there was no supper.

"Let's look in the other rooms," said Mother; and they looked. And in each room was the same kind of blundering half-arrangement of furniture, and fire-irons and crockery, and all sorts of odd things on the floor, but there was nothing to eat; even in the pantry there were only a rusty cake-tin and a broken plate with whitening mixed in it.

"What a horrid old woman!" said Mother; "she's just walked off with the money and not got us anything to eat at all."

"Then shan't we have any supper at all?" asked Phyllis, dismayed, stepping back on to a soap-dish that cracked responsively.

"Oh, yes," said Mother, "only it'll mean unpacking one of those big cases that we put in the cellar. Phil, do mind where you're walking to, there's a dear. Peter, hold the light."

The cellar door opened out of the kitchen. There were five wooden steps leading down. It wasn't a proper cellar at all, the children thought, because its ceiling went up as high as the kitchen's. A bacon-rack hung under its ceiling. There was wood in it, and coal. Also the big cases.

Peter held the candle, all on one side, while Mother tried to open the great packing-case. It was very securely nailed down.

1. What is meant by 'winky, blinky'? (Line 1)

Answer: 'Winky blinky' describes the <u>flickering</u> of the candlelight.

Have you seen how a candle flickers even when there isn't any draught? These words have come from the words, wink and blink- both are linked to eye movements. This is a metaphor of how a candle flame flickers back and forth, momentarily giving and taking light; just like blinking and winking obscures our sight for a split second.

2. Why was the dining room darker than the kitchen?

Answer: The kitchen was painted white while the dining room had dark wood on the walls. And there were black beams across the ceiling. This made the dining room darker. (Lines 5-7)

3. What does the underlined word mean in this phrase?

a) the kitchen was <u>whitewashed'</u> (Line 6)

Answer: Painted white

If you did not already know the meaning, let us look at the context.

The word whitewashed contains 'white' in it so it has to do with the colour white. Also, the darkness of the dining room is being compared with the kitchen; so, from the above two pieces of evidence, we can infer that it's referring to the colour of the paint.

b) 'His bad reputation was whitewashed'- what do you think this phrase means?

Answer: His bad reputation was covered up

In this context, the word is used as a <u>metaphor</u> to mean that something negative is covered up or hidden- just like **white paint** will cover over the marks and blemishes on a wall.

4. Who is referred to as a 'horrid woman'? What was she expected to do?
Answer: Mrs Viney is referred to as a horrid woman because she was asked to buy food and prepare supper for the family but she did not do so. (Line 3, 15 and 16)

5. What two words have been contracted to make the word **shan't**? (Line 17)
Answer: Shall and not

6. What evidence suggests that there was no electricity?
Answer: They were using candles.
There is reference to candles being lit and used at the beginning and the end of the text.

7. According to the children, what is a proper cellar like? Mention 2 things.
Answer: According to the children, a proper cellar should have a low ceiling and is usually small in size.
Be careful with this question as it is asking you for the opposite of what the children are seeing.
The text describes what the children see and they think to themselves that it isn't a proper cellar.
"It wasn't a proper cellar at all, the children thought, because its ceiling went up as high as the kitchen's. A bacon-rack hung under its ceiling. There was wood in it, and coal. Also the big cases." (Lines 21-23)
The question asks what a 'proper cellar' looks like according to the children's opinion. So a proper cellar would be the opposite of what they see.
- "because its ceiling went up as high as the kitchen's" therefore, a proper cellar must have a low ceiling.
- "...there was wood in it, and coal. Also the big cases."- This indicates the cellar was big as it contained lots of items; therefore, suggesting that proper cellars are small.

Peter Pan

Word match
a) Custom b) Lingering c) Stowing d) Sometimes e) Intensely f) Savages g) For instance h) Forsaken i) Delectable

Mind picture
As you read, did you imagine the setting?
Mrs Darling is putting her children to sleep, and as per her usual habit she goes through her children's minds to sort out their thoughts; thoughts that they have accumulated during the course of the day. She cherishes the good ones and puts away the not so good ones.
The extract then goes on to describe Neverland; where it can be found and what it looks like. It all sounds very magical and mystical.

Peter Pan

Published as a novel in 1911, 'Peter Pan' is J. M. Barrie's most famous work. The story is about a mischievous yet innocent little boy who can fly and has many adventures on the Island of Neverland that is inhabited by mermaids, fairies, Native Americans and pirates. Other characters include, Tinker Bell, Captain Hook, the Lost Boys, Wendy and her two brothers.
The extract below draws an image of what Neverland may look like.

Mrs Darling first heard of Peter when she was tidying up her children's minds. It is the nightly custom of every good mother after her children are asleep to rummage in their minds and put things straight for next morning, repacking into their proper places the many articles that have wandered during the day. If you could keep awake (but of course you can't) you would see your own mother doing this, and you would find it very interesting to watch her. It is quite like tidying up drawers. You would see her on her knees, I expect, lingering humorously over some of your contents, wondering where on earth you had picked this thing up, making discoveries sweet and not so sweet, pressing this to her cheek as if it were as nice as a kitten, and hurriedly stowing that out of sight. When you wake in the morning, the naughtiness and evil passions with which you went to bed have been folded up small and placed at the bottom of your mind and on the top, beautifully aired, are spread out our prettier thoughts, ready for you to put on.
I don't know whether you have ever seen a map of a person's mind. Doctors sometimes draw maps of

1. At what point of the day or night did Mrs Darling first hear of Peter Pan?
Answer: At night/ bedtime (Line 1-2)
Remember the question is asking at what point of the day/night, not what she was doing. So, it would be incorrect to write 'when she was tidying her children's mind'.

2. What is Mrs Darling tidying in her children's minds?
Answer: She is tidying her children's thoughts. (Lines 8-11)
Even if you missed the evidence, you could have made an educated guess; as we hold thoughts and ideas in our minds.

3. What simile is used to describe the action of tidying minds?
Answer: It is quite like tidying up drawers (Lines 3-6)

You can identify similes by the usage of 'like' or 'as'; they are used to draw comparisons between two things.

4. Based on the context give an example of:
a. Discoveries sweet (line 7)
Answer: A good thought
b. And not so sweet (line 7)
Answer: A bad thought

The text talks about the mother sorting through the child's thoughts and as she does, she cherishes the pleasant thoughts and hurriedly puts away the unpleasant, negative thoughts. So, a sweet discovery would represent a pleasant thought while a not so sweet discovery would be an unpleasant negative thought

5. Why is it not possible to see your own mother tidying your mind? (from the text)
Answer: It is not possible to see your own mother tidy your mind as it happens after you have fallen asleep. (Lines 3-4)

I don't know whether you have ever seen a map of a person's mind. Doctors sometimes draw maps of other parts of you, and your own map can become intensely interesting, but catch them trying to draw a map of a child's mind, which is not only confused, but keeps going round all the time. There are zigzag lines on it, just like your temperature on a card, and these are probably roads in the island, for the Neverland is always more or less an island, with astonishing splashes of colour here and there, and coral reefs and rakish-looking craft in the offing, and savages and lonely lairs, and gnomes who are mostly tailors, and caves through which a river runs, and princes with six elder brothers, and a hut fast going to decay, and one very small old lady with a hooked nose. It would be an easy map if that were all, but there is also first day at school, religion, fathers, the round pond, needle-work, murders, hangings, verbs that take the dative, chocolate pudding day, getting into braces, say ninety-nine, three-pence for pulling out your tooth yourself, and so on, and either these are part of the island or they are another map showing through, and it is all rather confusing, especially as nothing will stand still.

Of course, the Neverlands vary a good deal. John's, for instance, had a lagoon with flamingos flying over it at which John was shooting, while Michael, who was very small, had a flamingo with lagoons flying over it. John lived in a boat turned upside down on the sands, Michael in a wigwam, Wendy in a house of leaves deftly sewn together. John had no friends, Michael had friends at night, Wendy had a pet wolf forsaken by its parents, but on the whole the Neverlands have a family resemblance, and if they stood still in a row you could say of them that they have each other's nose, and so forth. On these magic shores children at play are for ever beaching their coracles [simple boat]. We too have been there; we can still hear the sound of the surf, though we shall land no more. Of all delectable islands the Neverland is the snuggest and most compact, not large and sprawly, you know, with tedious distances between one adventure and another, but nicely crammed. When you play at it by day with the chairs and table-cloth, it is not in the least alarming, but in the two minutes before you go to sleep it becomes very real. That is why there are night-lights.

6. What does the word intensely mean? (Line 13)

Answer:

Very/greatly/extremely etc.

If you didn't know what intensely means then try looking at the context.

"...and your own map can become intensely interesting".

Say the sentence without the word 'intensely' and see if it still makes sense.

Great, so it makes sense! So, what is the function of the word 'intensely'?

It's giving more detail to the adjective 'interesting'.

So, 'intensely' is an adverb.

Now try replacing the word 'intensely' with another adverb and see if it makes sense.

7. Why can it be difficult to draw a map of a child's mind?

Answer: (Any 2) It can be difficult to draw a child's mind because it is confusing/ it keeps going round/ it includes the vivid imagination of the child/ it contains thoughts about the child's life/ nothing stands still. (see line 13-23)

8. Where can Neverland be found?

Answer: In the imagination of every child

It doesn't explicitly say in the text, but there is plenty of evidence suggesting that it is in a child's imagination:

"but catch them trying to draw a map of a child's mind" (Line 13)

Here is a reference to Neverland being in the mind of children.

Neverland also includes imaginary thoughts and fantasy ideas as well as real-life occurrences such as school, religion, and fathers etc.; all of which are thoughts in a child's mind.

Neverland is different for each child:

"Of course the Neverlands vary a good deal. John's, for instance, had a lagoon with flamingos flying over it at which John was shooting, while Michael, who was very small, had a flamingo with lagoons flying over it" (Lines 24-26)

And finally, the text says that Neverland is in the imaginary games children play by day with chairs and table cloth and at night in the racing thoughts just before they fall asleep; suggesting that Neverland is in the imagination.

"When you play at it by day with the chairs and table-cloth, it is not in the least alarming, but in the two minutes before you go to sleep it becomes very real. That is why there are night-lights." (Lines 33-35)

Pinocchio: Master Antonio and the piece of wood

Word match

a) on account of b) Beamed c) Imploringly d) Evidently e) Tremendous f) Dolefully g) Recovered h) Mercy i) Fright

Mind picture

The scene takes place in Master Antonio's shop. There are tools and lots of wood as it is a woodshop. There may be wooden furniture and other items being made and sold. As it is a workshop, there may be lots of wood chips and sawdust all over the floor.

The main characters are Master Antonio, a carpenter and a piece of wood that makes human-like noises. This is an example of **anthropomorphism**- human characteristics in non-human objects

Pinocchio: Master Antonio and the piece of wood

Written in 1883 by Italian author Carlo Collodi, Pinocchio, is a fictional story about a puppet that comes to life.
In this piece the carpenter has a shock of his life when he discovers that a seemingly lifeless piece of wood begins to speak.

There was once upon a time a piece of wood in the shop of an old carpenter named Master Antonio. Everybody, however, called him Master Cherry, on account of the end of his nose, which was always as red and polished as a ripe cherry.
No sooner had Master Cherry set eyes on the piece of wood than his face beamed with delight, and, rubbing his hands together with satisfaction, he said softly to himself:
"This wood has come at the right moment; it will just do to make the leg of a little table."
He immediately took a sharp axe with which to remove the bark and the rough surface, but just as he was going to give the first stroke he heard a very small voice say imploringly, "Do not strike me so hard!"
He turned his terrified eyes all around the room to try and discover where the little voice could possibly have come from, but he saw nobody! He looked under the bench—nobody; he looked into a cupboard that

1. Why was Master Antonio referred to as Master Cherry?
Answer: His nose was red as a cherry. (Lines 2-3)

2. What did he plan on doing with the piece of wood?
Answer: Make the leg of a little table. (Line 6)

3. What does imploringly mean? (line 8) What effect does it have on the speech? (2)
Answer: To beg desperately. It adds the effect that the wood was pleading for its life.

If you did not know the meaning of implorinly, first look at the type of word it is: it is an adverb- (it describes how an action took place)
Now take a look at the sentence.
The wood says, "Do not strike me so hard!" Just before this is the word 'imploringly'. So, the word 'imploringly' tells us the manner in which the wood spoke.
Now, consider for yourself, the piece of wood is about to be struck by an axe; remember, the wood does not have any hands or feet to stop the strike so it calls out in *desperation*.
The adverb ***imploringly,*** tells us how it called out and adds the effect of begging/desperation.

And, taking up the axe, he struck a tremendous blow on the piece of wood.
"Oh! oh! you have hurt me!" cried the same little voice dolefully.
This time Master Cherry was petrified. His eyes started out of his head with fright, his mouth remained open, and his tongue hung out almost to the end of his chin, like a mask on a fountain. As soon as he had recovered the use of his speech he began to say, stuttering and trembling with fear:
"But where on earth can that little voice have come from that said 'Oh! oh!'? Is it possible that this piece of wood could have learned to cry and to lament like a child? I cannot believe it. This piece of wood is nothing but a log for fuel like all the others, and thrown on the fire it would about suffice to boil a saucepan of beans. How then? Can anyone be hidden inside it? If anyone is hidden inside, so much the worse for him. I will settle him at once."

4. What had happened to Master Cherry's speech for a short time? And why?
Answer: He was speechless due to the shock of hearing a piece of wood speak.
(Lines 17-19 and 20- 21)

5. Find 3 similes in the extract.

Answer: "cry and to lament like a child" (Line 21), "as red and polished as a ripe cherry" (Line 3), "as if he had been struck by lightning" (Line 34)

Similes are used to describe and compare something to another unrelated thing: i.e. it is not exactly the same, but there's some similarity.
The wood is compared to a child because of the action of crying and lamenting **like** human children sometimes do.
The red nose is compared to a cherry because of the **likeness** in colour.
He fell to the ground **as** if he was struck by lightning. He was not really, but the shock was 'shocking' like lightning.
You can often identify similes by the use of '**like**' and '**as**'.

> "But where on earth can that little voice have come from that said 'Oh! oh!'? Is it possible that this piece of wood could have learned to cry and to lament like a child? I cannot believe it. This piece of wood is nothing but a log for fuel like all the others, and thrown on the fire it would about suffice to boil a saucepan of beans. How then? Can anyone be hidden inside it? If anyone is hidden inside, so much the worse for him. I will settle him at once."
>
> So saying, he seized the poor piece of wood and commenced beating it without mercy against the walls of the room.
>
> Then he stopped to listen if he could hear any little voice lamenting. He waited two minutes—nothing; five minutes—nothing; ten minutes—still nothing!
>
> "I see how it is," he then said, forcing himself to laugh, and pushing up his wig; "evidently the little voice that said 'Oh! oh!' was all my imagination! Let us set to work again."
>
> Putting the axe aside, he took his plane, to plane and polish the bit of wood; but whilst he was running it up and down he heard the same little voice say, laughing:
>
> "Stop! you are tickling me all over!"
>
> This time poor Master Cherry fell down as if he had been struck by lightning. When he at last opened his eyes he found himself seated on the floor.
>
> His face was changed, even the end of his nose, instead of being crimson, as it was nearly always, had become blue from fright.

6. In the carpenter's mind, what is the most one could do with that piece of wood?

Answer: Boil a saucepan of beans. (Line 21-23)

It would about suffice: it would just be enough

7. Give two pieces of evidence that suggest that the log of wood is small

Answer: It will just do to make the leg of a little table. (Line 6)
It would about suffice to boil a saucepan of beans. (Line 22-23)

Leg of a little table suggests its small size. And, just about enough to boil a saucepan of beans suggest that it would not burn for long due to its size.

8. What does crimson mean? (line 36)

Answer: Deep red colour (Line 36-37)

Do you remember at the beginning of the text, the carpenter is described as having a red nose? Well, here it no longer is due to the fright he received from the wood.
The word 'instead' indicates the change from crimson to blue.
Therefore, we should be able to infer the meaning of crimson as red.

9. What caused the wood to laugh?

Answer: The carpenter was running the planer up and down the wood/ carpenter was polishing the wood. (Lines 31-33)

If you answered: 'the carpenter tickled the wood' you wouldn't get the mark. He did not start off by tickling it, rather it was the result of him polishing it and rubbing it up and down.

Helen Keller

Word match
a) Siblings b) Lineage c) Native d) Dense e) Obstacles f) Advised g) Uniquely h) Exhausted i) Series

This is a short biography- an account of someone's life written by another person.
An autobiography is an account of one's own life, written by themselves. It is non-fiction, so, it will be factual, based on actual incidents in the life of a person. Biographies will include important dates and names of people and places.

> ## Helen Keller
>
> This text is a biography of Helen Keller, it is non-fiction and gives an account of a person's life. Her life is an example of great achievements despite her disabilities.
>
> Helen Adams Keller was born on June 27, 1880, in Tuscumbia, Alabama. She had four siblings; two full siblings, and two older half-brothers from her father's prior marriage.
> Her father, Arthur Henley Keller spent many years as an editor of the Tuscumbia *North Alabamian* and had served as a captain in the Confederate Army. Her mother, Catherine Everett (Adams) Keller, was the daughter of Charles W. Adams. Her paternal lineage was traced to Casper Keller, a native of Switzerland.
> At 19 months old Keller contracted an unknown illness described by doctors as "an acute congestion of the stomach and the brain", which might have been scarlet fever or meningitis. The illness left her both deaf and blind. She lived, as she recalled in her autobiography, "at sea in a dense fog."
> At that time, Keller was able to communicate somewhat with Martha Washington, the six-year-old

1. How many children did Helen's father, Arthur Henley Keller have?
Answer: Five children. (Lines 1-2)
Don't forget to count Helen as well! Four siblings in addition to Helen makes five children.

2. List one of Helen's father's jobs
Answer: Editor of newspaper / Captain in the Confederate Army (Line 3-4)
The keywords in the question are 'Helen's father' and 'job'. However, you won't find 'job' in the text. So, first locate a reference to Helen's father and then see if you can find information about what he did.

3. What is Helen's maternal grandfather's name?
Answer: Charles W. Adams (Lines 4-5)
Keywords: maternal grandfather's name
Like the previous question, you won't find these words in the text, so, find the meaning of the words instead.
Maternal- relating to the mother's side.
Helen's mother's father, Charles W. Adams, is Helen's maternal grandfather.

4. What does lineage mean? (Line 5)
Answer: Ancestry/family
Scan the text until you find the word; the line number has been given for quick reference.
The whole paragraph is talking about family; and from the word '*paternal*' we know it is still talking about Helen's family -from the father's side.
The word 'traced' tells us it is going back- as in when you 'trace your steps back'. This tells us that our family that came before us are our ancestry and our lineage.

5. What does Helen mean by "at sea in a dense fog."? (Line 9)
Answer: This describes her inability to see and hear. The sea represents the isolation she possibly felt due to not being able to hear any more, and the fog represents her loss of eyesight. (something similar is acceptable)
Helen is deaf, so, depending on her level of deafness, she may only hear very loud noises and feel vibrations- comparing it to being at sea suggests that she can't hear much.
'Dense fog' suggests her inability to see comparing it to her blindness.

through many obstacles and she learned to live with her disabilities. She learned how to tell which person was walking from the vibrations of their footsteps.

In 1886, young Keller, accompanied by her father, was sent to seek out physician J. Julian Chisolm, an eye, ear, nose, and throat specialist in Baltimore, for advice. Chisholm referred the Kellers to Alexander Graham Bell, who was working with deaf children at the time. Bell advised them to contact the Perkins Institute for the Blind; the school's director asked 20year-old former student Anne Sullivan, herself visually impaired, to become Keller's instructor. It was the beginning of a 49year-long relationship during which Sullivan evolved into Keller's governess and eventually her companion.

Sullivan arrived at Keller's house on March 5, 1887, a day Keller would forever remember as *my soul's birthday*. Sullivan immediately began to teach Helen to communicate by spelling words into her hand, beginning with "d-o-l-l" for the doll that she had brought Keller as a present. Keller was frustrated, at first, because she did not understand that every object had a word uniquely identifying it. In fact, when Sullivan was trying to teach Keller the word for "mug", Keller became so frustrated she broke the mug. Keller's breakthrough in communication came the next month when she realized that the motions her teacher was making on the palm of her hand while running cool water over her other hand, symbolized the idea of "water". Writing in her autobiography, *The Story of My Life*, Keller recalled the moment. "I stood still, my whole attention fixed upon the motions of her fingers. Suddenly I felt a misty consciousness as of something forgotten — a thrill of returning thought; and somehow the mystery of language was revealed to me. I knew then that w-a-t-e-r meant the wonderful cool something that was flowing over my hand. The living word awakened my soul, gave it light, hope, set it free!" Keller then nearly exhausted Sullivan demanding the names of all the other familiar objects in her world.

In 1904, at the age of 24, Keller graduated from Radcliffe, becoming the first deaf-blind person to earn a Bachelor of Arts degree.

Helen wrote many books and articles. She travelled the world giving lectures to raise awareness and raised funds to help deaf and blind people.

Following a series of strokes, Helen spent the later part of her life at home. Helen died in her sleep on 1st June 1968. She was buried at the Washington National Cathedral in Washington, D.C.

6. How did Keller know who was walking?

Answer: From the vibrations of their footsteps. (Line 13-14)

This also tells us that each person had a different vibration and she could identify the person by the unique vibrations of their steps.

7. What / who is a physician?
Answer: Doctor

...was sent to seek out physician J. Julian Chisolm, an eye, ear, nose, and throat specialist in Baltimore, for advice. (Lines 15-16)
Considering Hellen's condition and the specialities of this physician (eye, ear, nose and throat) we can assume it must be a doctor or some sort of medical professional.

8. Who taught Helen how to communicate using sign?
Answer: Anne Sullivan (Line 22)

9. Did Anne Sullivan have any disabilities? If yes what was it?
Answer: yes, she was visually impaired.
20-year-old former student Anne Sullivan, herself visually impaired, (Lines 18-19)

Visually impaired- partially or completely blind
Anne also attended a special school for the blind.
Bell advised them to contact the Perkins Institute for the Blind; the school's director asked 20-year-old former student Anne Sullivan, herself visually impaired, to become Keller's instructor. (Lines 17-19)

10. What is meant by 'misty consciousness'?
Answer: A faint memory coming back (Lines 29-30)
This is an example of a metaphor- comparing something to another unrelated thing- returning thoughts as misty consciousness i.e. not vividly but vaguely due to the 'mist'.

11. Today, many people graduate from universities, why was it particularly special of Helen to graduate?
Answer: Helen's education must have been challenging due to her being blind and deaf unlike most people/ she overcame her challenges to earn the degree. (Line 35-36)
Helen was the first blind and deaf person to graduate. We already know the difficulties Helen experienced in her life due to her disabilities, therefore, earning a university degree would have been a great challenge which she succeeded at.

Alice in Wonderland

Word match

a) peeped b) conversations c) sleepy d) remarkable e) curiosity f) dipped g) disappointment h) wonder i) grand

ALICE was beginning to get very tired of sitting by her sister on the bank, and of having nothing to do: once or twice she had peeped into the book her sister was reading, but it had no pictures or conversations in it, "and what is the use of a book," thought Alice, "without pictures or conversations?"

So she was considering in her own mind (as well as she could, for the hot day made her feel very sleepy and stupid) whether the pleasure of making a daisy-chain would be worth the trouble of getting up and picking the daisies, when suddenly a White Rabbit with pink eyes ran close by her.

There was nothing so *very* remarkable in that; nor did Alice think it so *very* much out of the way to hear the Rabbit say to itself, "Oh dear! Oh dear! I shall be too late!" (when she thought it over afterwards, it occurred to her that she ought to have wondered at this, but at the time it all seemed quite natural); but when the Rabbit actually took a watch out of its waistcoat-pocket, and looked at it, and then hurried on, Alice started to her feet, for it flashed across her mind that she had never before seen a rabbit with either a waistcoat-pocket, or a watch to take out of it, and burning with curiosity, she ran across the field after it, and was just in time to see it pop down a large rabbit-hole under the hedge.

In another moment down went Alice after it, never once considering how in the world she was to get out again.

The rabbit-hole went straight on like a tunnel for some way, and then dipped suddenly down, so suddenly that Alice had not a moment to think about stopping herself before she found herself falling down what seemed to be a very deep well.

Either the well was very deep, or she fell very slowly, for she had plenty of time as she went down to look about her, and to wonder what was going to happen next. First, she tried to look down and make out what she was coming to, but it was too dark to see anything; then she looked at the sides of the well and noticed that they were filled with cupboards and book-shelves: here and there she saw maps and pictures hung upon pegs. She took down a jar from one of the shelves as she passed; it was labelled "ORANGE MARMALADE," but to her disappointment it was empty; she did not like to drop the jar for fear of killing somebody underneath, so managed to put it into one of the cupboards as she fell past it.

"Well!" thought Alice to herself. "After such a fall as this, I shall think nothing of tumbling down stairs! How brave they'll all think me at home! Why, I wouldn't say anything about it, even if I fell off the top of the house!" (Which was very likely true.)

Down, down, down. Would the fall *never* come to an end? "I wonder how many miles I've fallen by this time?" she said aloud. "I must be getting somewhere near the centre of the earth. Let me see: that would be four thousand miles down. I think—" (for, you see, Alice had learnt several things of this sort in her lessons in the schoolroom, and though this was not a very good opportunity for showing off her knowledge, as there was no one to listen to her, still it was good practice to say it over) "—yes, that's about the right distance—but then I wonder what Latitude or Longitude I've got to?" (Alice had no idea what Latitude was, or Longitude either, but thought they were nice grand words to say.)

1. Why was Alice not interested in her sister's book?

Answer: It didn't have any pictures or conversations (Line 3). Seems like a book for older children or even adults due to the lack of pictures. It may also be a non-fiction book as it does not contain any conversations between characters (which is usually a common feature of fiction books).

2. What caused Alice to feel lazy and unable to concentrate?

Answer: The heat/ hot weather (Lines 4-5)

The words 'lazy' and 'unable to concentrate' are not used in the extract. However, 'sleepy' can be related to feeling lazy; and 'stupid' can be related to being unable to concentrate.

3. Find a metaphor. (Lines 11-13)

Answer: 'burning with curiosity' (Line 12)

This is an example of a metaphor which is a type of figurative speech. It suggests that the curiosity to find out was 'burning' (extreme).

a. What does this metaphor mean?

Answer: Intense desire to find out

The curiosity (urge to know) is so intense it is described as burning.

4. Why would Alice not say anything to anyone even if she fell off the top of the house?

Answer: it is less important than falling down the very deep well. / The well is so deep that the top of a house does not feel too high to fall from. (Line 26-28)

5. Find an example of a simile.

Answer: Like a tunnel (Line 16)

Simile: an expression comparing one thing to another. Contains words- 'like' and 'as'. - The rabbit-hole is compared to a tunnel.

6. Give 2 possible reasons why Alice had time to think as she was falling

Answer: It was a deep well. She was falling slowly. (Lines 19-20)

7. Why was it not a good opportunity to show off Alice's knowledge?

Answer: There was no one to listen to her. (Lines 32-33) Showing off can only be effective when there are other people to see or hear.

8. a) What use do we have with longitude and latitude? Search online if you need to. **Answer**: They are used to find any location on the earth

b) Which subject or area of knowledge would you commonly find these words? **Answer**: Geography (Geography is the study of the features of earth and its atmosphere.)

Little Women

Word match- a) contentedly b) altered c) proposed d) manner e) libel f) satirical g) dignity h) fretting i) reproving

"Christmas won't be Christmas without any presents," grumbled Jo, lying on the rug.

"It's so dreadful to be poor!" sighed Meg, looking down at her old dress.

"I don't think it's fair for some girls to have plenty of pretty things, and other girls nothing at all," added little Amy, with an injured sniff.

"We've got Father and Mother, and each other," said Beth contentedly from her corner.

The four young faces on which the firelight shone brightened at the cheerful words, but darkened again as Jo said sadly, "We haven't got Father, and shall not have him for a long time." She didn't say "perhaps never," but each silently added it, thinking of Father far away, where the fighting was.

Nobody spoke for a minute; then Meg said in an altered tone, "You know the reason Mother proposed not having any presents this Christmas was because it is going to be a hard winter for everyone; and she thinks we ought not to spend money for pleasure, when our men are suffering so in the army. We can't do

1. Why did Meg say it is dreadful to be poor?

Answer: Because they could not afford presents. (Lines 1-2)
From what Jo is saying we can see that she is unhappy as they will probably not get any presents for Christmas. Additionally, we know from Meg's sighing and looking down at her old dress that they are poor.

2. Where is father?

Answer: Fighting in the army/ At war (Line 8, 11)

3. On line 9, 'Meg said in an altered tone': what has the **tone** altered to?

Answer: A positive tone/ Non- complaining

Alter means to change something- 'altered tone' – 'different tone'

At the beginning of the text Meg is speaking in a complaining manner:

'"It's so dreadful to be poor!" sighed Meg' (Line 2), complaining about her lack of money for presents.

Followed by:

then Meg said in an altered tone, "You know the reason Mother proposed not having any presents this Christmas was because it is going to be a hard winter for everyone; and she thinks we ought not to spend money for pleasure, when our men are suffering so in the army. (Lines 9-11) - 'altered' from the initial complaint.

And finally, Meg reverts back to her original complaining tone again:

"I know I do—teaching those tiresome children nearly all day, when I'm longing to enjoy myself at home," began Meg, in the complaining tone again. (Line 23-24)

I do want to buy *Undine and Sintran* for myself. I've wanted it so long," said Jo, who was a bookworm.

"I planned to spend mine in new music," said Beth, with a little sigh, which no one heard but the hearth brush and kettle-holder.

"I shall get a nice box of Faber's drawing pencils; I really need them," said Amy decidedly.

"Mother didn't say anything about our money, and she won't wish us to give up everything. Let's each buy what we want, and have a little fun; I'm sure we work hard enough to earn it," cried Jo, examining the heels of her shoes in a gentlemanly manner.

"I know I do—teaching those tiresome children nearly all day, when I'm longing to enjoy myself at home," began Meg, in the complaining tone again.

"You don't have half such a hard time as I do," said Jo. "How would you like to be shut up for hours with a nervous, fussy old lady, who keeps you trotting, is never satisfied, and worries you till you're ready to fly out the window or cry?"

"It's naughty to fret, but I do think washing dishes and keeping things tidy is the worst work in the world. It makes me cross, and my hands get so stiff, I can't practice well at all." And Beth looked at her rough hands with a sigh that anyone could hear that time.

"I don't believe any of you suffer as I do," cried Amy, "for you don't have to go to school with impertinent girls, who plague you if you don't know your lessons, and laugh at your dresses, and label

4. What are *Undine and Sintram*? Try figuring it out from the text.

Answer: Books/ Magazines/ Something for reading (Line 16)
The word 'bookworm' tells us that Jo is fond of reading, so, Undine and Sintran must be the name of a book, magazine or some other reading material.
Also, consider that the words are capitalised and written in italics. Titles of books can sometimes be written in italics.

5. Were the King children rich?

Answer: Yes

...the King children, for they were fighting and fretting all the time, in spite of their money. (Lines 41-42)

'In spite of their money' is the same as 'even though they had money'.

"So I did, Beth. Well, I think we are. For though we do have to work, we make fun of ourselves, and are a pretty jolly set, as Jo would say."

"Jo does use such slang words!" observed Amy, with a reproving look at the long figure stretched on the rug.

Jo immediately sat up, put her hands in her pockets, and began to whistle.

"Don't, Jo. It's so boyish!"

"That's why I do it."

"I detest rude, unladylike girls!"

"I hate affected, niminy-piminy chits!"

Adapted from *Little Women* by Louisa May Alcott

6. Why were the girls happier than the King children?

Answer: They have a good sense of humour as they can make fun of themselves. They were cheerful. (Lines 43-44)

7. What makes Jo boyish?

Answer: Her use of slang, putting her hands in her pocket and whistling. (Lines 45, 47-48)

8. Use a dictionary and find the appropriate meaning of the word **'chit'** as it is used in line 51.

Answer: An immature or childish girl.

Check in a dictionary and select the most appropriate word. You'll find that only one definition fits

heels of her shoes in a gentlemanly manner.

"I know I do—teaching those tiresome children nearly all day, when I'm longing to enjoy myself at home," began Meg, in the complaining tone again.

"You don't have half such a hard time as I do," said Jo. "How would you like to be shut up for hours with a nervous, fussy old lady, who keeps you trotting, is never satisfied, and worries you till you're ready to fly out the window or cry?"

"It's naughty to fret, but I do think washing dishes and keeping things tidy is the worst work in the world. It makes me cross, and my hands get so stiff, I can't practice well at all." And Beth looked at her rough hands with a sigh that anyone could hear that time.

"I don't believe any of you suffer as I do," cried Amy, "for you don't have to go to school with impertinent girls, who plague you if you don't know your lessons, and laugh at your dresses, and label your father if he isn't rich, and insult you when your nose isn't nice."

9. What are the girls' jobs/or daily activities? What do they do during the day?

Answer: Meg- teacher (Line 23-24), Jo- looks after an old lady(Lines 25-27), Beth- does housework/chores(Lines 28-30), Amy- goes to school(Lines 31-32.

King Arthur's Knights

Word match - a) marvel b) strange c) angry d) tournament e) fetch f) obtain g) grasped h) forth i) covetous

Mind picture/ context

This story is set in medieval Britain.

The characters are kings, lords and other notables who are intrigued by the prospect of pulling the sword out. Think of a movie scene from King Arthur or any other movie set in that era.

The main characters in this extract are Arthur and Sir Kay. Arthur is described as a boy who doesn't seem to have much interest in the sword but would rather be taking part in the merriment of the jousts.

King Arthur's Knights

This story is based in 6th century England; a time of kings, queens, knights and magicians. So, you will find some unfamiliar words and references that may sound strange to you. But try to guess the meaning from the context. As you read don't forget to draw an image in your mind and try to imagine yourself there.

In this extract people discover the sword in the stone; they try to pull it out to claim the prize of becoming the king.

The clerk ran into the church and told the archbishop, and men were all amazed and would have gone instantly to see this marvel, but the archbishop bade them stay.

'Finish your prayers to God,' he said, 'for no man may touch this strange thing till high Mass be done.' When Mass was finished, all poured forth from the church and thronged about the stone, and marvelled at the words on the sword. First King Lot, with a light laugh, took hold of the handle and essayed to pull out the point of the sword, but he could not, and his face went hot and angry. Then King Nentres of Garlot took his place with a jest, but though he heaved at the sword with all his burly strength, till it seemed like to snap, he could not move it, and so let go at last with an angry oath. All the others essayed in like manner, but by none was it moved a jot, and all stood about discomfited, looking with black looks at one another and the stone.

'He that is right wise born ruler of Britain is not here,' said the archbishop at length, 'but doubt not he shall come in God's good time. Meanwhile, let a tent be raised over the stone, and do ye lords appoint ten of your number to watch over it, and we will essay the sword again after New Year's Day.'

So that the kings and lords should be kept together, the archbishop appointed a great tournament to be held on New Year's Day on the waste land north of the city, which men now call Smithfield.

Now when the day was come, a certain lord, Sir Ector de Morven, who had great lands about the isle of Thorney, rode towards the jousts with his son, Sir Kay, and young Arthur, who was Sir Kay's foster-brother. When they had got nearly to the place, suddenly Sir Kay bethought him that he had left his sword at home.

'Do you ride back, young Arthur,' he said, 'and fetch me my sword, for if I do not have it I may not fight.' Willingly Arthur turned his horse and rode back swiftly. But when he had arrived at the house, he found it shut up and none was within, for all had gone to the jousts. Then was he a little wroth, and rode back

1. What is ***Mass*** as it appears in the text? (Line 4) Choose the correct answer.

Answer: d) A form of Religious worship (Lines 3-4)

If you look at the text, you can see reference to church and prayers.

From the multiple-choice selection, you can see there is an option related to religion.

Also, notice the capital letter on the word 'Mass'. This means it has to be a proper noun; not the common noun- mass (A large body of matter with no definite shape).

2. What does the word essay/essayed mean as used in the text? (Lines 5 - 13)

Answer: To try /Attempt

If you didn't know already, try looking at the context. Everyone is eager to pull the sword out of the stone, so they're all '*trying*'.

Now have a look and try replacing it with another suitable word

3. When Arthur went back to get the sword, why was no anyone at home?

   Answer: Everyone was at the jousts. (Line 21-22)

4. What does the word **wroth** mean? (line 22) Select the correct answer

   angry annoyed happy sad

   Answer: Angry

If you look at the context you will see that Arthur had ridden all the way back to his home but no one was in, so this made him angry. How would you feel in this situation?

NOTE: There are other options which could also fit, (annoyed or sad), however, try to put yourself in that situation and see which emotion/word would fit the best.

Sometimes you just won't be able to be 100% sure. Try your best and make an educated guess. Don't leave any question unanswered.

*Educated guess- an opinion based upon judgement, some knowledge and after narrowing down the options.

'Do you ride back, young Arthur,' he said, 'and fetch me my sword, for if I do not have it I may not fight.'

Willingly Arthur turned his horse and rode back swiftly. But when he had arrived at the house, he found it shut up and none was within, for all had gone to the jousts. Then was he a little wroth, and rode back wondering how he should obtain a sword for his foster-brother.

Suddenly, as he saw the tower of St. Paul's church through the trees, he bethought him of the sword in the stone, about which many men had spoken in his hearing.

'I will ride thither,' said he, 'and see if I may get that sword for my brother, for he shall not be without a sword this day.'

When he came to the churchyard, he tied his horse to the stile, and went through the grave-mounds to the tent wherein was the sword. He found the place unwatched, and the flashing sword was sticking by the point in the stone.

Lightly he grasped the handle of the sword with one hand, and it came forth straightway!

Then, glad that his brother should not be without a sword, he swiftly gat upon his horse and rode on, and delivered the sword to Sir Kay, and thought no more of aught but the splendid knights and richly garbed lords that were at the jousts.

But Sir Kay looked at the sword, and the writing, and knew it was the sword of the stone, and marvelled how young Arthur had possessed himself thereof; and being of a covetous and sour mind he thought how he might make advantage for himself. He went to his father, Sir Ector, and said:

'Lo, father, this is the sword of the stone, and surely am I rightful king.'

5. '...he swiftly **gat** upon his horse and rode on' (Line 32).
What does the highlighted word mean?

Answer: Got

Look at the sentence, what is he doing? He got onto his horse.

Gat - Archaic (old English) past tense of 'get'.

6. How were the lords dressed at the jousts?

Answer: They were dressed in fine clothing/ Wearing their best clothes. (lines 33-34)

7. What does 'Lo' mean? (Line 38)

Answer: Look

This is old English and is used to grab someone's attention or to look at something interesting.

'Lo and behold'- literally means – 'look and see'

This phrase is also used in modern language as an *idiom* to say when something **surprising** happens or in sarcasm.

'I was minding my own business when, lo and behold, John turns up...'

'I'd been looking for my pen for ages when, lo and behold, it was in my pocket the whole time.'

Can you tell the difference between the surprised expression and the sarcastic one?

8. Did Arthur know about the sword in the stone from before?

Answer: Yes

a. How do you know?

Answer: It says in the text that he had heard men talking about it. (Lines 24-25)

9. How would you describe Sir Kay? Select two

cunning selfless selfish honest

Answer: Cunning, Selfish

The extract shows you how Sir Kay was desirous of the sword and its kingship. It shows how he planned to take advantage for his own gain- cunning and selfish. (Lines 35-38)

Pinocchio and the Cricket

Word match- a) fastened b) a hundred years c) woe d) rebel e) escape f) impertinence g) vagabond h) rage i) scarcely

Mind Picture/context

The main characters in this text are Pinocchio and Cricket. This is an example of anthropomorphism. Cricket advises Pinocchio not to run away. However, he doesn't heed the advice; instead he is rude to Cricket and in a fit of rage ends up hurting him. The text includes persuasive and advisory language from Cricket, while Pinocchio responds arrogantly.

1. What does ajar mean? (Line 1)

Answer: Slightly open

The information in Line 1 suggests that the door must have been unlocked and slightly open for him to be able to push it open fully and walk in.

> Arriving at the house he found the street door ajar. He pushed it open, went in, and having fastened the latch, threw himself on the floor and gave a great sigh of satisfaction.
>
> But soon he heard someone in the room who was saying:
>
> "Cri-cri-cri!"
>
> "Who calls me?" said Pinocchio in a fright.
>
> "It is I!"
>
> Pinocchio turned round and saw a big cricket crawling slowly up the wall.
>
> "Tell me, Cricket, who may you be?"
>
> "I am the Talking-Cricket, and I have lived in this room a hundred years or more."
>
> "Now, however, this room is mine," said the puppet, "and if you would do me a pleasure go away at once, without even turning round."
>
> "I will not go," answered the Cricket, "until I have told you a great truth."
>
> "Tell it me, then, and be quick about it."
>
> "Woe to those boys who rebel against their parents and run away from home. They will never come to any good in the world, and sooner or later they will repent bitterly."
>
> "Sing away, Cricket, as you please, and as long as you please. For me, I have made up my mind to run away tomorrow at daybreak, because if I remain I shall not escape the fate of all other boys; I shall be sent to school and shall be made to study either by love or by force. To tell you in confidence, I have no wish to learn; it is much more amusing to run after butterflies, or to climb trees and to take the young birds out of their nests."
>
> "Poor little goose! But do you not know that in that way you will grow up a perfect donkey and that everyone will make fun of you?"

2. Why is Cricket written with a capital letter?

Answer: It is used as a proper noun

The word cricket is a common noun and does not need to be capitalised. However, here the author has capitalised it suggesting that it is the actual name of the cricket. We can see both examples in the extract below:

Pinocchio turned around and saw a big cricket crawling slowly up the wall. (Line 7) -Used as a common noun.

"Tell me, Cricket, who may you be?" (Line 8) – Addressing the Cricket by its proper name

3. Which literary devise is used in this book with reference to the characters?

Answer: Anthropomorphism

Anthropomorphism is when a writer gives human traits to animals and non-human objects. In this book, Pinocchio is a wooden puppet that behaves like a boy and the cricket is given human characteristics such as speech and wisdom.

4. What animal is referenced to indicate someone not very smart?

Answer: Donkey

In some cultures around the world, people consider the donkey to be stubborn and hard to work with; so, as a result, people who are stubborn, ignorant or awkward may be referred to as a donkey. If you did not know this, then let's find clues in the text itself.

"I have no wish to learn; it is much more amusing to run after butterflies, or to climb trees and to take the young birds out of their nests." (Line 18-20)

"Poor little goose! But do you not know that in that way you will grow up a perfect donkey, and that everyone will make fun of you?" (Lines 21-22)

Pinocchio tells the Cricket that he will run away because he doesn't want to go to school. So, the Cricket responds by saying he'll grow up to be a donkey. Following this statement, he adds that everyone will make fun of Pinocchio.

"Tell it me, then, and be quick about it."
"Woe to those boys who rebel against their parents and run away from home. They will never come to any good in the world, and sooner or later they will repent bitterly."
"Sing away, Cricket, as you please, and as long as you please. For me, I have made up my mind to run away tomorrow at daybreak, because if I remain I shall not escape the fate of all other boys; I shall be sent to school and shall be made to study either by love or by force. To tell you in confidence, I have no wish to learn; it is much more amusing to run after butterflies, or to climb trees and to take the young birds out of their nests."
"Poor little goose! But do you not know that in that way you will grow up a perfect donkey and that everyone will make fun of you?"
"Hold your tongue, you wicked, ill-omened croaker!" shouted Pinocchio.
But the Cricket, who was patient and philosophical, instead of becoming angry at this impertinence, continued in the same tone:
"But if you do not wish to go to school why not at least learn a trade, if only to enable you to earn honestly a piece of bread!"
"Do you want me to tell you?" replied Pinocchio, who was beginning to lose patience. "Amongst all the

5. What does woe mean?

Answer: Great sorrow

This is an old English term used to talk about great misfortune, misery, sorrow, sadness etc.

"Woe to those boys who rebel against their parents and run away from home." (Line 14)

Replace the word 'woe' with the word 'misfortune.'

'Misfortune upon those boys who rebel against their parents and run away from home.'

6. What is Pinocchio trying to escape from by running away?

Answer: He is escaping the fate of all other boys/avoiding having to go to school/ from having to study. (Lines 17-18)

7. What other option does Cricket give Pinocchio? And why?

Answer: A) He is told to learn a trade. B) To get a job and feed himself. (Line 26-27)

Earn a piece of bread is to get work to feed oneself.

8. Describe the Cricket in terms of behaviour and characteristics.

Answer: Old, wise, patient (any 2)

Remember to look at the marks given. This will tell you how much to answer.

"...and I have lived in this room a hundred years or more." (Line 9)

"But the Cricket, who was patient and philosophical, instead of becoming angry..." (Line 24)

Because you are a puppet and, what is worse, because you have a wooden head.
At these last words Pinocchio jumped up in a rage and, snatching a wooden hammer from the bench, he threw it at the Talking-Cricket.
Perhaps he never meant to hit him, but unfortunately it struck him exactly on the head, so that the poor Cricket had scarcely breath to cry "Cri-cri-cri!" and then he remained dried up and flattened against the wall.
Pinocchio by Carlo Collodi

9. What happened to Cricket after he was hit?

Answer: He died.

Lines 40-42: Cricket is struck on the head, he struggles to breathe, and he remained dried up on the wall.

Healthy breakfasts (for people who hate breakfast)

Word match- a) whet b) habitual c) tempt d) eat e) chores f) comforting g) classic h) simmer i) spoon

Context

This is an article from the NHS website. It is non-fiction and is written in the second person; it aims to **encourage and persuade** the reader of the benefits of eating a healthy breakfast. The article also includes a list of ingredients and step by step instructions on how to make porridge.

Get into the habit of eating a morning meal with these simple breakfasts, designed to whet the appetite of even the most habitual breakfast-skipper.

Not hungry first thing in the morning? Pushed for time? Trying to lose weight? These calorie-counted treats will tempt you to rediscover the pleasure of breakfast.

From energy-boosting "apple pie" porridge and protein-packed scrambled eggs to a nutrient-rich green smoothie and granola bars, there's something for everyone.

"Creating the habit of eating in the morning is something you can build towards," says dietitian Alison Hornby. "Start off with a light bite, such as a piece of fruit or low-fat yoghurt.

"After a while, your morning appetite will naturally increase, and you'll probably find you eat less throughout the day, including snacks."

Research suggests people who eat breakfast are slimmer because they tend to eat less during the day – particularly fewer high-calorie snacks.

1. What does the word habitual mean? (line 2))

   Answer: To do something regularly.

   If you didn't already know:

a. find the root word within 'habitual'. It's 'habit'.
b. So, it is the word 'habit' with the suffix *'ual'*- this tells us it is something to do with an action/activity we do regularly.
c. And the suffix, *ual,* turns nouns into adjectives.

This now tells us that it is a word used to describe something or someone that does something regularly.
Now, if you are uncertain about the suffix, you could take an educated guess from the root word (habit), and you should come to the answer: 'doing something regularly'.

2. What does 'whet the appetite' mean?

   Answer: Increase the desire for food

'...these simple breakfasts, designed to whet the appetite of even the most habitual breakfast-skipper' (Line 1-2)
Firstly, let's remind ourselves of the objective of this text. It is written to persuade people who do not eat breakfast to start a new habit of eating.
Secondly, let us deconstruct the sentence.
"The most habitual breakfast-skipper"- some people do not eat breakfast – the problem.
"These simple breakfasts (have been) designed" – tells us what has been done to solve the problem.
"Whet the appetite"- increase the desire for food.
"These simple breakfasts (have been) designed to *increase the desire for food* of even the most habitual breakfast-skipper."
In a dictionary, you'll find other meanings such as:
Whet- to sharpen a knife, tool or weapon
to arouse/ excite/increase/strengthen one's interest/desire in food/knowledge

"Whetting one's appetite" - this phrase is also an idiom which means – to increase the desire to have or do something.

3. In the above article, there is only one recipe, which word/phrase tells you that there were more recipes?

   Answer: These calorie-counted treats

There is only one recipe in this extract; however the word 'these' (Line 1) suggests there were more in the original article.
These calorie-counted treats will tempt you to rediscover the pleasure of breakfast. (Lines 3-4)

4. What habit will cause your appetite to increase?

   Answer: Eating in the morning. (Lines 7-9)

5. Why are breakfast eaters slimmer?

   Answer: Because they eat less during the day. (Lines 11-12)

From energy-boosting "apple pie" porridge and protein-packed scrambled eggs to a nutrient-rich green smoothie and granola bars, there's something for everyone.

"Creating the habit of eating in the morning is something you can build towards," says dietitian Alison Hornby. "Start off with a light bite, such as a piece of fruit or low-fat yoghurt.

"After a while, your morning appetite will naturally increase, and you'll probably find you eat less throughout the day, including snacks."

Research suggests people who eat breakfast are slimmer because they tend to eat less during the day – particularly fewer high-calorie snacks.

If you're short on time in the morning, think about ways to keep your breakfast choice simple. You could also try waking up 10 minutes earlier or getting other chores out of the way ahead of time.

Energy-boosting breakfasts

'Apple pie' porridge

Serves: 1 adult
Preparation time: 10 minutes
Cooking time: 5 minutes
Calories per portion: 315kcal (1,318kJ)

Ingredients

50g porridge oats
200ml semi-skimmed milk
1 medium dessert apple, diced
Pinch of cinnamon

This is a warm, comforting porridge spiced up with the classic flavours of a homemade apple pie.

Throw all the ingredients into a saucepan. Heat and stir until boiling, then lower the heat and simmer gently for 5 minutes, stirring often.

Spoon the porridge into a serving bowl and add a sprinkle of cinnamon.

6. Find an example of alliteration. (Lines 4-9)
Answer: Protein-packed (Line 5)

Alliteration: When closely connected words begin with the same letter or sound.
e.g. bouncy bunny, swimming sea lion, she sells seashells on the seashore.

7. What does the word simmer mean?
Answer: To heat until just below boiling point.
"Heat and stir until boiling, then lower the heat and simmer gently for 5 minutes" (Lines 27-28)
Here is evidence that after boiling you bring the temperature down to 'simmer,' i.e. just before it boils.

8. If you are short of time, what two things could you do to help you have breakfast?
Answer: Keep breakfast simple/ wake up earlier/ do chores beforehand

Printed in Poland
by Amazon Fulfillment
Poland Sp. z o.o., Wrocław

53848540R00036